100 AMAZING FACTS ABOUT DOLPHINS

Index

"While we strive to understand dolphins, we are actually learning to understand ourselves."

- Thomas I. White

Introduction

Welcome to the fascinating world of dolphins! These intelligent, playful sea creatures have captured the human imagination for centuries. But beyond their charming appearance, dolphins hide a multitude of secrets and surprising behaviors that you'll discover throughout these pages. Get ready to plunge into the world of these extraordinary animals.

Through this book, you'll explore 100 incredible facts about dolphins, from the most well-known to the most surprising. Each Fact will reveal a unique aspect of their lives, from their incredible intelligence and ingenious hunting techniques to their amazing social interactions. Whether you're passionate about marine life or just curious, these facts will open up a whole new perspective on these fascinating marine mammals.

Dolphins are much more than just aquatic creatures. Their ability to communicate, play, help each other and even develop relationships with other species is simply incredible. They live in complex societies, use tools and are highly adaptable. This book will help you understand why they are considered one of the most intelligent species in the animal kingdom.

Browsing through these pages, you'll realize just how remarkable creatures dolphins are, capable of feats that often defy our understanding. This book isn't just a collection of facts; it's an invitation to admire, respect and protect these ambassadors of the oceans. Each Fact is a window on their mysterious world, a world you can discover in detail.

Prepare to be amazed by these 100 incredible facts about dolphins. Whether you're at the beach, in an aquarium, or just at home, let yourself be transported to the depths of the ocean and discover the secrets of these amazing animals. This book is a celebration of the beauty, intelligence and diversity of dolphins. Enjoy your journey into their fascinating world!

Marc Dresqui

Fact 1 - Dolphins breathe consciously even in their sleep

Unlike most mammals, dolphins have to think about every breath they take. In fact, their breathing is not an automatic reflex as it is in humans. When you sleep, your body breathes without you having to think about it. But for dolphins, it's different. They have to remain partially conscious, even when asleep, to be able to surface and breathe. This means that dolphins have conscious control over their breathing, which is essential for their survival in the water.

To understand how dolphins breathe while they sleep, you need to know that they don't sleep like you. Instead of plunging into a deep, complete sleep, dolphins sleep with only one half of their brain at a time, while the other half remains awake. This type of sleep is called unihemispheric sleep. While one half of the brain is at rest, the other controls breathing and watches out for potential dangers. After about two hours, the roles are reversed, and the other half of the brain rests. This method enables dolphins to remain alert while sleeping.

One of the most fascinating examples of this phenomenon was observed in captive dolphins, where researchers were able to see how these animals alternate between the two hemispheres of their brains. This not only enables them to breathe regularly, but also to monitor their environment, in particular to avoid predators or stay in contact with members of their group. This shows just how well adapted dolphins are to their aquatic environment.

The Fact that dolphins must consciously control their breathing also has implications for their behavior. For example, when moving over long distances, dolphins can alternate between periods of sleep and wakefulness while remaining on the move. They are able to maintain a high level of activity without ever entering a deep sleep as humans do. This enables them to cover vast distances without endangering themselves.

Dolphins' conscious sleep illustrates their exceptional ability to adapt to marine life. By controlling their breathing even during sleep, these animals can navigate the oceans while remaining alert. This unique adaptation is one of the many wonders of the animal kingdom, and a testament to the incredible complexity of dolphins.

Fact 2 - Dolphins use names to recognize each other

Dolphins have a remarkable ability that sets them apart from most other animals: they use "names" to identify themselves. This name is not a word like we use them, but a unique whistle that serves as a personal identifier. Each dolphin develops its own whistle from an early age, a little like you do when you learn your first name. This whistle then becomes a kind of vocal signature, recognizable by the other members of its group.

Studies carried out by researchers have shown that when two dolphins meet, they exchange whistles, as if they were greeting each other using their respective names. For example, if a dolphin hears the whistle of a companion it knows, it may respond by imitating that whistle to signal that it has recognized the other. This behavior shows not only that dolphins have an exceptional auditory memory, but also that they understand the importance of identity in their social interactions.

A fascinating example of this ability was observed in dolphins living in the waters of the Bahamas. Scientists recorded and analyzed the whistles of several dolphins and discovered that each whistle was as unique as a fingerprint. When a dolphin was separated from its pod and later reintroduced, it used its signature whistle to signal its return, and the other dolphins responded with their own whistles, as if welcoming a long-lost friend.

This ability to use names shows what intelligent, social creatures dolphins are. The Fact that they can remember and use the whistles of other dolphins proves the existence of deep social bonds within their groups. Dolphins don't just live together, they maintain complex relationships in which each individual is recognized and respected for his or her unique identity.

Dolphin communication goes far beyond the simple exchange of sounds. Their ability to use names demonstrates a form of awareness of self and others, a rare characteristic in the animal kingdom. This is one of the many reasons why dolphins are considered one of the most intelligent species on the planet, with social interactions that continue to fascinate scientists and observers the world over.

Fact 3 - Dolphins can swim at 55 km/hr

Dolphins are among the fastest marine animals, capable of swimming at impressive speeds of up to 55 km/h. This speed is achieved thanks to their bodies, which are perfectly adapted to life in the water. Their slender, hydrodynamic silhouette, combined with smooth skin, enables them to move through the water with minimal resistance. When you observe a dolphin in full race, you'll notice that it almost seems to fly underwater, using all its muscular power to propel its body at incredible speeds.

Dolphins don't swim fast just to impress. It's a vital survival skill. When hunting, dolphins use their speed to pursue and capture fast prey such as flying fish or mackerel. In the Atlantic Ocean, for example, dolphins can hunt in groups, encircling a school of fish and forcing them into a dense mass. Then, in a fraction of a second, they dive at full speed to capture their meal.

Dolphins' ability to swim fast is also crucial for escaping predators. Sharks, which pose a threat to dolphins, can sometimes be outrun thanks to this speed. In the event of danger, a dolphin may suddenly accelerate, rapidly changing direction to avoid an attack. This type of rapid maneuvering is often observed in situations where dolphins need to react instantly to avoid a predator or to protect each other within their group.

Scientists studied the speed of dolphins using various technologies, such as GPS tracking and underwater cameras. They discovered that these animals use not only their muscular strength, but also special techniques such as jumping out of the water to reduce resistance and increase their speed. These jumps, known as "porpoising", enable dolphins to cover great distances quickly, by combining underwater swimming with leaps into the air.

This ability to swim at 55 km/h is a testament to the dolphins' adaptation to their marine environment. Not only does it enable them to hunt efficiently and escape predators, it is also a demonstration of the beauty and power of these incredible creatures. Watching them in full race is a fascinating spectacle, revealing all the grace and efficiency of their anatomy.

Fact 4 - Dolphins recognize themselves in a mirror

One of the most fascinating discoveries about dolphin intelligence is their ability to recognize themselves in a mirror. This recognition test is often used by scientists to assess self-awareness in animals. Dolphins, like great apes and some birds, have been shown to possess this rare ability. When a dolphin is placed in front of a mirror, it does not react as if it were seeing another dolphin. Instead, it uses the mirror to explore its own body, sometimes making specific movements to check its reflection.

This ability has been demonstrated in several captive experiments. For example, researchers marked dolphins with non-toxic stains on parts of their bodies that they couldn't see without the aid of a mirror. When then exposed to a mirror, the dolphins inspected these marks, a behavior that shows they understand that the reflection in the mirror is their own image. This kind of test is a clear demonstration of self-awareness, a characteristic once thought to be reserved for humans and a few other highly intelligent species.

The Fact that dolphins can recognize themselves in a mirror suggests that they have a high level of self-awareness, comparable to that of human children from the age of 18 months. This self-awareness is linked to complex behaviors such as empathy, planning, and perhaps even a form of understanding of the past and future. For example, a dolphin that recognizes itself in a mirror might also be able to understand that its actions have consequences, and that other dolphins have perspectives different from its own.

The implications of this discovery are far-reaching. It means that dolphins are able to reflect on themselves, to see themselves as distinct individuals with their own thoughts and experiences. This recognition in the mirror could also explain why dolphins have such complex social behaviors, and why they are able to establish lasting relationships with other individuals, whether of the same species or even other species.

Fact 5 - A dolphin can understand 60 human commands

Dolphins are renowned for their exceptional intelligence, and one of the most striking proofs of this is their ability to understand and execute human commands. When trained, dolphins can learn to respond to over 60 different commands. These commands can vary from simple movements, such as jumping out of the water, to more complex actions, such as picking up a specific object or performing a series of movements in a precise order.

Dolphins' ability to understand commands is the result of a learning process that relies on visual and aural cues. For example, a trainer may use hand gestures, whistles or even words to communicate with a dolphin. What's remarkable is that dolphins don't just react mechanically. They are able to distinguish subtle differences in signals and understand the context in which these commands are given.

A famous example of this ability comes from studies carried out in the 1970s by researchers working with captive dolphins. They discovered that dolphins could not only learn a large number of commands, but could also understand complex concepts such as "object to the right" or "red object". This shows that dolphins not only memorize actions, but can also understand spatial relationships and specific characteristics of objects.

This ability to understand numerous commands also demonstrates that dolphins have excellent memory and cognitive flexibility. They can recall learned commands long after their initial training, and are able to apply acquired knowledge to new situations. For example, a dolphin that has learned to jump through a ring could understand how to jump through another similar object without the need for further training.

Dolphins' ability to understand 60 or more commands illustrates not only their intelligence, but also the depth of their relationship with humans. They are able to collaborate closely with their trainers, demonstrating an understanding and receptiveness that far exceeds that of most other animals. This skill is further proof that dolphins are among the most intelligent and communicative creatures in the animal kingdom.

Fact 6 - Dolphins have unique voiceprints

Dolphins possess an extraordinary ability: each individual develops a unique "vocal imprint", much like human fingerprints. These vocal imprints, often called signature whistles, are distinct sounds that each dolphin creates and uses to identify itself to other members of its group. From birth, young dolphins begin to develop these whistles, which become their personal sound identity for the rest of their lives.

Scientists discovered this ability by recording and analyzing communications between dolphins. They found that each signature whistle is unique to the individual producing it. When a dolphin hears its own whistle played back on tape, it often responds by repeating that whistle, showing that it recognizes the sound as its own. What's more, when dolphins greet each other or reunite after a separation, they use these whistles to re-identify each other, just as we would when calling someone by their first name.

A striking example of this ability has been observed in wild dolphin groups. When members of a group are dispersed over a wide area of the ocean, they use their signature whistles to maintain contact and come together again. This demonstrates not only the practical function of these whistles for navigation and communication, but also the importance of social bonds in dolphins. Signature whistles enable dolphins to stay connected, even in environments where visibility is limited.

This unique vocal imprint is essential for dolphins' social interactions. It enables them to recognize each other individually, and to establish and maintain complex relationships within their group. Dolphins can even memorize and recognize the whistles of dolphins they haven't seen for years, proving the existence of long-term memories and advanced social intelligence.

Dolphins' signature whistles are a fascinating aspect of their communication. They illustrate not only the complexity of their social interactions, but also the way in which these intelligent marine animals perceive and organize their world. Each dolphin's unique vocal imprint testifies to their individuality and the importance of social relationships in their daily lives.

Fact 7 - Dolphins have been helping fishermen since Antiquity

The relationship between dolphins and humans goes back thousands of years, and in some parts of the world, these marine animals have played a crucial role in fishing activities. As far back as antiquity, there are accounts of dolphins actively helping fishermen to catch fish. These well-documented collaborations testify to the intelligence and sociability of dolphins, as well as their ability to establish cooperative links with humans.

A famous example of this cooperation comes from the shores of ancient Greece. Greek fishermen observed that dolphins chased schools of fish towards their nets, facilitating their capture. In return, the dolphins benefited from the fishing by catching the fish that escaped from the nets. This win-win partnership is one of the oldest testimonies to inter-species collaboration, and has been immortalized in many of the region's myths and legends.

This tradition of fishing with dolphins still exists today in some parts of the world. In the Brazilian town of Laguna, for example, local fishermen cooperate with dolphins in a very specific way. The dolphins push the fish towards the shore, then give a signal to the fishermen by slapping the water with their tails. The fishermen then know it's time to cast their nets. This practice, handed down from generation to generation, demonstrates the mutual understanding and communication between dolphins and humans.

Why dolphins choose to help fishermen remains partly a mystery, but it underlines their high intelligence and ability to understand the benefits of collaboration. The dolphins participating in these fisheries have also shown an ability to remember the specific techniques and signals used by the fishermen, proving their ability to learn and adapt to human behavior.

These interactions between dolphins and fishermen are a fascinating illustration of how two species can coexist and cooperate for a common benefit. They demonstrate not only the social complexity of dolphins, but also their ability to form alliances with very different species, enriching our understanding of their intelligence and social behavior.

Fact 8 - The albino dolphin is extremely rare

The albino dolphin is one of the rarest and most fascinating marine creatures to observe. Albinism in dolphins, as in other animals, is due to a lack of pigment in the skin and eyes, giving them an all-white or very pale appearance. Albino dolphins are so rare that every sighting is considered an exceptional event by scientists and marine life enthusiasts.

One of the most famous examples of an albino dolphin is a bottlenose dolphin nicknamed "Pinky", which was first spotted in the waters of the Calcasieu River in Louisiana, USA. Pinky caught the public's attention because of its unusual pale pink color, which is due to a slight transparency of the skin allowing blood vessels to show through. This particular dolphin was observed for several years, becoming a veritable local celebrity and arousing the interest of researchers to better understand the implications of albinism in cetaceans.

Albino dolphins often face additional challenges compared to their fellow dolphins. Their lack of pigmentation makes them more vulnerable to the sun's UV rays, which can lead to sunburn and other skin problems. What's more, their eyes, also lacking pigment, are more sensitive to light, which can affect their vision. Despite these challenges, some albino dolphins manage to live long lives in their natural habitat, like Pinky, who has survived far beyond what one would expect of an albino dolphin.

The appearance of an albino dolphin in the wild is so rare that each sighting is carefully documented by scientists. These rare dolphins offer a unique opportunity to study genetic variation within dolphin populations, and to understand how albinism can affect their behavior and interaction with their environment. However, due to their rarity, there is still much to learn about the lives of albino dolphins in the wild.

The albino dolphin, with its distinct color and genetic peculiarities, remains a symbol of the diversity and beauty of the animal world. Each appearance of these rare animals is a reminder of the complexity and diversity of marine life, and the importance of protecting and studying these unique creatures to better understand the mysteries of the ocean.

Fact 9 - Dolphins can use sponges as tools

Dolphins are not only known for their intelligence and sociability, but also for their ability to use tools, a rare skill among animals. One of the most fascinating examples of this ability is the use of marine sponges by some dolphins to protect themselves when searching for food. This practice was first observed in female dolphins from the Shark Bay pod in Australia, and quickly captured the attention of scientists.

When these dolphins dive to the bottom of the sea in search of food, they run the risk of injuring themselves by digging through coral and sharp rocks. To avoid this, some of them detach sponges from the seabed and place them on their rostrum (snout), using the sponge as a kind of protective glove. This technique enables them to search for prey buried in the sand without the risk of cutting themselves or pricking themselves on dangerous marine organisms, such as sea urchins.

The use of sponges by Shark Bay dolphins is a behavior that seems to be culturally transmitted, mainly from mother to daughter. This means that it is not an innate skill, but one that is learned and taught. This cultural transmission is an extremely rare phenomenon in animals, and shows just how capable dolphins are of complex behavior and social learning. Young dolphins observe their mothers and imitate this technique until they have mastered it themselves.

The researchers also noted that this use of tools is not universal among all dolphins, but limited to certain populations, reinforcing the idea of cultural learning specific to certain groups. What's more, this practice appears to be particularly beneficial in environments where food is harder to come by, demonstrating the adaptability and ingenuity of dolphins in the face of environmental challenges.

Dolphins' use of sponges is a striking example of their ability to solve problems creatively. This behavior reminds us that dolphins are not only intelligent animals, but also innovators, capable of adapting their environment to their needs by using objects in sophisticated ways. This discovery continues to intrigue scientists and broaden our understanding of dolphins' cognitive abilities.

Fact 10 - Dolphins are inter-species friends

Dolphins are renowned for their sociability and intelligence, and these qualities are not limited to interactions with fellow dolphins. They are also capable of forming friendly relationships with other marine species, and even with humans. These inter-species relationships go beyond mere chance encounters, demonstrating dolphins' exceptional ability to establish emotional and cooperative bonds with animals of other species.

One of the most famous examples of this inter-species relationship is the enduring friendship between dolphins and humpback whales. In some areas, it is not uncommon to see dolphins swimming in the company of whales, playing around them and accompanying them on their migrations. This behavior does not seem to be motivated by foraging or protection, but rather by the pleasure of interaction. Despite their imposing size, the whales tolerate and even encourage these games, creating a real sense of camaraderie.

Another illustration of these inter-species relationships is the interaction between dolphins and dogs. There are several accounts of dolphins approaching the coast to play with dogs swimming or running along the beach. These encounters, though brief, show that dolphins are curious and friendly, ready to interact playfully with creatures they've never met before. This demonstrates a certain openness and willingness to bond with very different species.

Dolphins have also been known to rescue other animals in distress. For example, dolphins have been reported to aid sea turtles by helping them right themselves when stuck on their backs, or even pushing sharks away from other endangered animals. These altruistic behaviors testify to their ability to recognize and respond to the needs of other species, which is extremely rare in the animal kingdom.

These friendly inter-species relationships show just how social dolphins are, capable of empathy and affection even towards animals very different from themselves. Their ability to forge bonds beyond the boundaries of their own species continues to fascinate researchers and observers alike, further revealing the complexity and richness of their social lives. These special interactions illustrate the extent of dolphins' awareness and intelligence, making them natural ambassadors for the ocean.

Fact 11 - Dolphins communicate with complex whistles

Dolphins are highly social creatures, and their communication relies on a sophisticated system of complex whistles. Each dolphin possesses a vocal repertoire that enables it to convey a variety of messages, from personal identification to the coordination of group movements. These whistles are not mere sounds; they form an elaborate language, adapted to the needs of community life.

These complex whistles can contain information about the dolphin's identity, location and even its emotional state. For example, a dolphin may emit a particular whistle to signal its presence to other members of the group, while another whistle may be used to warn of danger. This language is so precise that dolphins can even communicate at great distances, as the whistles propagate efficiently through the water.

A remarkable example of the complexity of these whistles was observed during research carried out on bottlenose dolphins. Scientists recorded and analyzed these whistles, discovering that each individual subtly modifies the pitch, duration and frequency of its sounds to express different messages. Sometimes, these whistles are so complex that they are reminiscent of the phrases we use to communicate, although they are obviously very different from our human language.

Whistling also plays a crucial role in coordinating group activities, such as hunting. For example, when dolphins hunt together, they use whistles to organize their strategy, to ensure that each member of the group knows where to position himself, and to synchronize their actions. This level of coordination shows that whistling is much more than a simple communication tool; it is essential to the survival and success of dolphins in their environment.

This ability to emit and interpret complex whistles demonstrates the intelligence and sociability of dolphins. Their vocal communication is not only a means of conveying information, but also an expression of their rich and interconnected social life. Dolphins thus demonstrate that they possess an elaborate form of language, which continues to fascinate researchers and broaden our understanding of the cognitive capacities of marine animals.

Fact 12 - Dolphins hunt in organized groups

Dolphins are exceptional hunters, and one of their most effective strategies is to hunt in organized groups. Unlike many other marine animals, dolphins do not hunt alone; they prefer to join forces to increase their chances of success. This collective behavior demonstrates not only their intelligence, but also their ability to cooperate closely to achieve a common goal.

When hunting in groups, dolphins use a method called "circling". They form a circle around a school of fish, pushing them towards the center as they swim in ever-tighter spirals. This technique disorients the fish and prevents them from escaping, leaving them vulnerable to the dolphins at the center of the circle. Then, each dolphin takes turns to feed, ensuring that all members of the group get their share of food.

A famous example of this collective hunt takes place in Florida waters, where dolphins often hunt in groups along the coast. They work together to group fish close to shore, where they are easier to catch. In some cases, the dolphins even use specific whistles to coordinate their movements, ensuring that each member of the group knows exactly what to do and when to do it.

This group hunting behavior is not only a matter of efficiency, but also of survival. Working together, dolphins can capture larger or faster prey than they could alone. This allows them to maximize their energy intake with less effort, which is crucial to their well-being. What's more, this group strategy strengthens the social bonds between dolphins, as it requires constant communication and mutual trust.

Hunting in organized groups is a testament to the social and cognitive complexity of dolphins. It shows how these animals use not only their intelligence to solve problems, but also their ability to work as a team to ensure their survival. This collective behavior is one of the many reasons why dolphins are considered one of the most intelligent and socially sophisticated species in the ocean.

Fact 13 - Dolphins can leap up to 5 meters

Dolphins are famous for their spectacular leaps out of the water, a behavior that continues to fascinate marine observers. What many people don't know is that these incredibly agile animals are capable of leaping up to 5 meters in the air, equivalent to the height of a two-storey building. These jumps, also known as "breaching", are not only impressive, they play a crucial role in the lives of dolphins.

One of the main roles of these jumps is related to communication and navigation. By jumping out of the water, a dolphin can get a better view of its environment, spotting obstacles, prey or members of its group. It also enables them to transmit signals to other dolphins, as the noise produced by the leap back into the water is audible over long distances. This behavior is particularly useful in murky waters or when hunting in groups, where underwater visibility may be limited.

These impressive leaps are also used for practical reasons, such as getting rid of parasites. By leaping high into the air and then hitting the water hard as it falls back, a dolphin can loosen crustaceans or algae clinging to its skin. This behavior, which combines strength and agility, shows just how well adapted dolphins are to their marine environment, using their bodies efficiently to maintain their health.

Researchers have also observed that dolphins seem to jump for pleasure. These jumps, sometimes in series, are often accompanied by games and pirouettes. This demonstrates the intelligence and playful nature of dolphins, which sometimes seem to jump simply for fun, to play with the waves, or even to interact with boats and humans observing them. This behavior adds to the image of dolphins as joyful, social creatures, capable of finding pleasure in everyday activities.

Finally, these jumps also enable dolphins to cover long distances quickly by combining swimming and gliding, enabling them to move through the water with great efficiency. Jumps from a height of 5 meters are therefore not only a sight to behold, but also a testament to the adaptability and inexhaustible energy of dolphins. These marine acrobatics continue to captivate those lucky enough to observe them, revealing the grace and power of these incredible marine mammals.

Fact 14 - The Amazon dolphin lives in fresh water

The Amazonian dolphin, also known as the boto or pink dolphin, is one of the few dolphins to live exclusively in freshwater. Unlike its marine cousins, this dolphin has adapted its way of life to the rivers and streams of the Amazon, a region rich in biodiversity. This unique aquatic mammal is particularly renowned for its pinkish color, which becomes more intense with age, giving it a distinctive appearance among dolphins.

The habitat of the Amazonian dolphin is mainly in the calm, shallow waters of the Amazon and Orinoco basins. These dolphins have developed special adaptations to survive in this complex environment. For example, they have extremely flexible necks, enabling them to navigate easily between the submerged roots and trunks of trees in flooded forests. This flexibility, rare in dolphins, enables them to capture prey in confined spaces where other predators cannot go.

Another fascinating feature of the Amazonian dolphin is its ability to live in waters where visibility is often severely reduced by turbidity. To compensate for this lack of visibility, these dolphins rely on their advanced echolocation, emitting clicks that bounce off surrounding objects to create a "sound image" of their surroundings. This ability enables them to detect and hunt fish, crabs and even turtles in conditions where vision is almost useless.

The Amazon dolphin's way of life is also closely linked to the Amazon flood cycle. During the rainy season, when rivers overflow and flood the vast forests, these dolphins explore new areas, hunting in previously inaccessible places. This seasonal adaptation is essential to their survival, as it enables them to follow the movements of fish, their main source of food, as they migrate with the floods.

The Amazon dolphin is not only a remarkable example of adaptation to a unique environment, it also plays a vital role in the region's ecosystem. As a top predator, it helps maintain the balance of fish populations and other aquatic species.

Fact 15 - Dolphins have a matriarchal social structure

Dolphins are social animals, living in groups where the social structure is often matriarchal. This means that females play a central role in the organization and stability of the group. In these societies, female dolphins are not only responsible for the protection and upbringing of their young, but they also influence collective decisions, such as movements and hunting strategies. This matriarchal organization is crucial to the survival of dolphin groups, as it ensures effective transmission of the knowledge and skills required for life in the marine environment.

An important aspect of this matriarchal structure is the strong bond between mothers and offspring. Young dolphins spend several years at their mother's side, learning to hunt, communicate and interact with other members of the pod. This extended learning period enables the young to acquire the skills needed to survive independently. In addition, older females, often called matriarchs, play an essential role as guides and protectors for younger members of the group.

Matriarchs, in particular, are respected for their experience and knowledge of migration routes, hunting grounds and social behaviors. For example, in some dolphin populations, matriarchs lead groups on seasonal movements to food-rich areas. The knowledge they have accumulated over the years is essential to the survival of the group, and their influence is felt in almost all collective decisions.

This matriarchal social structure also promotes strong cohesion within the group. Females form lasting alliances, often based on kinship relationships, which reinforce solidarity and cooperation between group members. These alliances can extend over several generations, as dolphins have an exceptional memory for maintaining complex relationships over long periods. This female solidarity contributes to the stability and resilience of dolphin groups in the face of environmental challenges.

Fact 16 - Dolphins sleep with one eye open

Dolphins have developed a unique sleeping method that enables them to stay alert while resting. Unlike humans, who plunge into a deep, complete sleep, dolphins sleep with only one half of their brain at a time. Meanwhile, the other half remains active, enabling them to continue monitoring their environment and maintaining vital functions such as breathing. One of the most fascinating aspects of this sleep is that dolphins often keep one eye open, further evidence of their alert state even when at rest.

This phenomenon, known as unihemispheric sleep, is crucial to the survival of dolphins. By keeping part of their brain awake, they can react quickly to potential dangers, such as the approach of a predator or sudden changes in their environment. What's more, this type of sleep enables them to control their breathing, which is essential for an animal that must regularly surface to breathe. So, even in a state of rest, a dolphin can continue to swim slowly and remain aware of what's going on around it.

Scientists have observed this behavior in captive dolphins, where they have found that dolphins alternate sleep periods between the two hemispheres of their brains. For example, if the left side of the brain is asleep, the right eye remains open, and vice versa. This process allows the dolphins to recuperate while remaining constantly on guard. This regular alternation between the two sides of the brain ensures that the dolphin remains alert and ready to react, even during periods of rest.

This sleeping mode is particularly advantageous in a marine environment where threats can arise at any moment. For example, a sleeping dolphin could be approached by a shark or other predator. By keeping one eye open, it can detect these dangers in time and react accordingly, either by fleeing or by alerting other members of its pod. This level of constant vigilance is one of the many examples of dolphins' adaptability to their habitat.

Dolphins' unihemispheric sleep is a testament to their extraordinary adaptation to aquatic life. This ability to sleep while remaining partially awake enables them to survive in an environment where vigilance is essential.

Fact 17 - The common dolphin can live up to 50 years

The common dolphin, or Delphinus delphis, is one of the most widespread and well-known species of dolphin. This marine mammal, with its slender body and contrasting colors, is often seen playing in the waves or swimming alongside boats. But what is less well known is that the common dolphin can live up to 50 years under the right conditions, making it one of the longest-lived dolphins in the world.

This longevity is largely due to the social nature of common dolphins, who live in groups called shoals, sometimes consisting of several hundred individuals. These groups offer protection from predators, but also opportunities to learn and pass on knowledge between generations. Young dolphins learn from their elders not only how to hunt, but also how to avoid danger and navigate their vast marine environment. This transmission of knowledge is essential to their long-term survival.

Common dolphins are also highly adaptable, which contributes to their longevity. They can live in a variety of marine environments, from shallow coastal waters to deeper ocean areas. Their varied diet, consisting mainly of fish and squid, enables them to adapt to different ecological conditions. This ability to adjust to changes in their environment is crucial to their long-term survival, especially in ever-changing oceans.

Another key factor in the longevity of common dolphins is their remarkable intelligence. Able to solve complex problems, communicate effectively with fellow dolphins and even form alliances with other species, common dolphins use their intelligence to avoid danger and maximize their chances of survival. For example, they can adjust their hunting behavior according to the season or local conditions, enabling them to maintain a regular diet throughout their lives.

The common dolphin's ability to live up to 50 years is a testament to its resilience and adaptation to its environment. This longevity, rare among marine mammals, underlines the importance of protecting marine habitats to ensure that these fascinating creatures can continue to thrive in our oceans for generations to come. Common dolphins, with their exceptional longevity, remain a living symbol of the richness and diversity of marine life.

Fact 18 - Dolphins play with boat waves

Dolphins are naturally playful animals, and one of their favorite activities is surfing the waves created by boats. This behavior, often observed by sailors and passengers alike, reveals not only the dolphins' agility, but also their penchant for play and interaction with their environment. When a boat moves, it creates a series of waves at the bow and stern, which the dolphins use to propel themselves at high speed without expending much energy.

The phenomenon is particularly visible when dolphins gather around large moving ships. They position themselves strategically in the waves generated by the bow, then let themselves be carried along by the force of the water. These waves allow them to glide gracefully across the surface of the water, often leaping and spinning, creating a fascinating spectacle for those lucky enough to observe them. This behavior is not only a demonstration of their agility, but also an example of their ability to find pleasure in activities that are, for other species, purely functional.

Scientists believe that this play with boat waves could have several functions. On the one hand, it could simply be a form of entertainment, a way for the dolphins to relax and have fun. On the other hand, it could also serve to strengthen social bonds within the group, as dolphins surfing together share a common experience that reinforces their cohesion. Young dolphins, in particular, seem to learn a lot from observing and imitating adults in these water games.

A notable example of this behavior has been observed off the coast of California, where dolphins regularly follow fishing boats and cruise ships. They often appear without warning, attracted by the movement of the water, and immediately begin to play in the bow waves, before the amazed eyes of the passengers. This interaction is a testament to the intelligence and curiosity of dolphins, who actively seek ways to interact with their environment, even when it involves man-made objects.

This cheerful, lively behavior shows that dolphins don't just survive in their environment, they turn it into a playground.

Fact 19 - Dolphins help the wounded in their group

Dolphins are not only social creatures, but also deeply empathetic, as demonstrated by their behavior when a member of their group is injured. When a dolphin is in difficulty, whether due to injury or illness, the other dolphins in its group do not hesitate to come to its aid. This altruistic behavior is particularly evident when a dolphin is having difficulty swimming or coming to the surface to breathe.

A poignant example of this solidarity was observed by researchers in New Zealand, where an injured dolphin was surrounded by several members of his pod. These dolphins took it in turns to push the injured dolphin to the surface, enabling it to breathe steadily. Without this help, the dolphin would not have survived, as it would not have been able to maintain its position at the surface on its own. This type of behavior shows not only cooperation within the group, but also a high level of social awareness.

Injured or sick dolphins often receive ongoing support from their companions, who may stay by their side for long periods. Sometimes this involves slowing the pace of the group to ensure that the injured dolphin can keep up. This kind of behavior has been documented in several dolphin populations around the world, illustrating that it is not an isolated phenomenon, but a common feature of the species.

This support is not limited to physical care. The dolphins also seem to offer emotional support to their injured fellow dolphins. They make specific sounds and rub against each other, gestures that seem to soothe and comfort the dolphin in distress. These behaviors recall the deep bonds that exist between members of a dolphin group, where each member's individuality is recognized and respected.

Helping injured dolphins demonstrates their ability to form complex social relationships based on empathy and cooperation. This trait distinguishes them as one of the most intelligent and socially sophisticated species in the animal kingdom. By caring for their fellow creatures, dolphins demonstrate that they possess not only practical intelligence, but also a sensitivity that enriches their social life and enables them to survive in an often difficult environment.

Fact 20 - Dolphins hunt using bubbles

Dolphins are ingenious hunters, using a variety of techniques to capture their prey. One of the most fascinating methods they employ is the use of bubbles to trap fish. This strategy, often referred to as "bubble netting", demonstrates the intelligence and cooperation of dolphins in their quest for food. By hunting in this way, they create a circle of bubbles around a school of fish, effectively enclosing and disorientating them, making them much easier to catch.

The process begins when one or more dolphins swim in a circle around a group of fish, releasing a series of bubbles through their blowholes. These bubbles quickly rise to the surface, forming a visible, impenetrable barrier for the fish. Disoriented by this barrier, the fish gather in a tight cluster, an instinctive response to what they perceive as a threat. It is precisely this reaction that the dolphins are waiting for.

Once the fish are trapped, the dolphins take it in turns to dive to the center of the circle to capture their meal. This type of hunting requires exceptional coordination and clear communication between group members. Everyone must play their part with precision for the technique to work. This is an excellent example of how dolphins use their collective intelligence to improve their hunting efficiency.

This technique has been observed in several dolphin populations around the world, including bottlenose dolphins in Florida and on the coast of Australia. This behavior is not innate but learned, which means that it is culturally transmitted from one dolphin to another, often from mother to calf. This cultural transmission further underlines the social intelligence of dolphins and their ability to develop complex strategies for solving everyday problems.

The bubble net not only demonstrates the ingenuity of dolphins, but also their ability to use elements of their environment to achieve their goals. By manipulating air bubbles, a naturally available resource, dolphins demonstrate a form of creativity rare in the animal kingdom, placing them among the ocean's most skilful and innovative predators.

Fact 21 - Dolphins feel complex emotions

Dolphins are not only intelligent animals, they are also capable of feeling complex emotions, a trait that brings them even closer to humans. These emotions go far beyond simple instinctive responses; they include feelings such as joy, sadness, affection, and even grief. Observations of dolphin behavior in their natural habitat and in captivity reveal a rich emotional life that plays a central role in their social dynamics.

A poignant example of these complex emotions is the grief dolphins feel when a member of their pod dies. It has been observed that mother dolphins sometimes carry their dead calf for several days, refusing to abandon it. They support it at the surface to allow it to "breathe", even though they know, on some level, that the calf will not come back to life. This behavior shows a deep emotional attachment and difficulty in accepting loss, a response that reflects an understanding of death and the sadness that accompanies it.

Dolphins also express joy in highly visible ways, including play and lively social interaction. When happy, they jump out of the water, swim with increased energy, and emit a series of rapid whistles and clicks. These behaviors are not only manifestations of physical pleasure, but also expressions of contentment and happiness, often shared with members of their group. These moments of collective joy strengthen social bonds and contribute to the overall well-being of the group.

Dolphins' emotions also play a role in their ability to form lasting relationships with other individuals, be they dolphins or even humans. Friendships between dolphins are often very strong and can last a lifetime.

The fact that dolphins feel complex emotions only adds to their reputation as extraordinary animals. This ability to experience and express deep feelings shows that their intelligence goes far beyond simple problem-solving, encompassing an emotional dimension that makes them even more fascinating and touching for those lucky enough to observe them.

Fact 22 - Dolphins and orcas are in the same family

Dolphins and orcas, although very different in appearance and size, actually belong to the same biological family: the delphinidae. This family comprises some 90 species of cetacean, including dolphins, killer whales and other small cetaceans such as pilot whales and white-sided dolphins. This relationship explains why orcas, often referred to as "killer whales", share so many behavioral and social characteristics with dolphins.

Orcas, despite their imposing size of up to 9 meters in length, are in fact the largest members of the dolphin family. Their behavior is remarkably similar to that of smaller dolphins, especially when it comes to their social organization. Like dolphins, killer whales live in groups called pods, often led by a dominant female. These pods are made up of extended families, where members cooperate to hunt, protect each other and raise young, just like dolphin groups.

Another thing dolphins and orcas have in common is their exceptional ability to communicate. Both species use a variety of sounds, including whistles, clicks and complex songs to coordinate and maintain group cohesion. Orcas, like dolphins, have also shown signs of a pod-specific culture, with specific hunting techniques and behaviors passed down from generation to generation, underlining the importance of social learning in these species.

The intelligence of orcas and dolphins is another trait they share. Both are capable of solving complex problems, creating alliances, and even manipulating their environment to get what they want. For example, some killer whale populations hunt by creating waves to knock seals off ice blocks, a sophisticated technique that demonstrates an advanced understanding of physics and cooperation.

The Fact that dolphins and orcas are from the same family illustrates not only the diversity of this cetacean family, but also the impressive abilities that link them. Whether through their intelligence, their complex social structure, or their ability to communicate, orcas and dolphins show that they share a common heritage that makes them among the most fascinating creatures in the ocean.

Fact 23 - The dolphin is an intelligent marine mammal

The dolphin, one of the most intelligent marine mammals, fascinates scientists and the general public alike with its exceptional cognitive abilities. As a mammal, the dolphin shares many characteristics with humans, such as the need to breathe air, the presence of hair at a developmental stage, and the way it feeds its young with milk. However, what particularly sets the dolphin apart from other marine animals is its remarkable intelligence, comparable to that of the great apes.

Dolphins are capable of solving complex problems, learning new skills, and passing on this knowledge to other members of their group. For example, they have been observed using tools such as marine sponges to protect their rostrum when searching for food on the seabed. This behavior, learned and transmitted from mother to daughter, demonstrates not only a capacity for innovation, but also a culture specific to certain dolphin populations.

Communication is another area where dolphin intelligence shines. They use a wide range of sounds, including whistles, clicks and snaps, to exchange information with each other. Each dolphin has a unique signature whistle, equivalent to a name, which it uses to identify and recognize itself among others. This ability to name themselves and maintain complex communications is further proof of their self-awareness and rich social life.

Dolphins are also capable of empathetic behavior, another indication of their intelligence. They show signs of compassion, for example by helping injured members of their pod to the surface to breathe, or by caring for orphaned calves. This complex emotional dimension demonstrates that dolphin intelligence is not limited to practical tasks, but also includes social and emotional aspects.

The dolphin is a marine mammal that combines physical traits adapted to aquatic life with an intelligence that rivals that of many other animals. Their ability to learn, communicate and feel emotions makes dolphins not only fascinating creatures to observe, but also important subjects of study for understanding the evolution of intelligence and sociability in the animal kingdom.

Fact 24 - Dolphins travel in groups called schools

Dolphins are social animals, spending most of their lives in groups. These groups, called schools, can vary considerably in size, from a few individuals to several hundred, depending on the species and environmental conditions. Living in schools offers dolphins many advantages, including protection, hunting and ocean navigation. This complex social organization is essential to their survival and well-being.

Schools of dolphins are often made up of members of the same family, with mothers, calves and sometimes close adult males. This family structure enables dolphins to share resources and protect the most vulnerable. For example, when predators such as sharks approach, the dolphins gather in a circle around the young, with the adults forming a protective barrier. This cooperative behavior shows just how vital social relationships are for dolphins.

Cooperation within schools is not limited to protection. When hunting, dolphins use coordinated strategies to capture their food. For example, they may encircle a school of fish, pushing them towards the center where they are easier to catch. This technique, which requires perfect synchronization between group members, is an excellent example of dolphins' collective intelligence. Schools also enable dolphins to exchange information on the best places to find food, reinforcing their success as hunters.

In addition to their practical role, benches are also centers of social interaction and play. Dolphins spend much of their time socializing, playing and strengthening bonds within their group. These playful interactions, which include running, jumping and chasing, are crucial to group cohesion and the development of young dolphins. Schools are therefore not only survival units, but also dynamic communities where dolphins develop and maintain complex relationships.

Dolphin schools are a perfect illustration of the importance of social relationships in these marine mammals. By living in groups, dolphins benefit from increased protection, more efficient hunting and a rich social life. This schooling is just one of the many adaptations that have enabled dolphins to become one of the ocean's most successful and fascinating species.

Fact 25 - Dolphins jump to observe their environment

Dolphins are well known for their spectacular leaps out of the water, but these acrobatics are not just a demonstration of their agility. In fact, these leaps enable them to observe their surroundings beyond the water's surface. By leaping into the air, dolphins can spot potential threats, locate schools of fish, or even assess the position of other members of their group. This technique, known as "spyhopping" when they poke their heads out of the water to observe, demonstrates their ability to use different senses to navigate and survive.

When dolphins jump, they take the opportunity to scan the horizon. This gives them a quick glimpse of what's going on around them, which they wouldn't get by staying underwater. For example, a dolphin leaping out of the water may spot an approaching boat, a potential predator such as a shark, or another pod of dolphins. This overview enables them to make strategic decisions about their next move, whether it's to head towards a food-rich area or away from imminent danger.

This behavior is particularly useful in environments where underwater visibility is reduced, such as in turbid waters or overgrown with vegetation. By emerging from the water, dolphins can obtain valuable visual information that complements their echolocation, giving them a complete picture of their environment. It's an adaptation that underlines their intelligence and ability to maximize the use of their senses to meet the challenges of their habitat.

The scientists also observed that dolphins sometimes jump in groups, which could enhance visual communication between them. By jumping simultaneously or in succession, they can share information about what they see above the surface. This collective behavior could be particularly important when hunting, where good coordination is essential for circling and capturing prey.

Dolphins' leaps to observe their environment are therefore not just a matter of play or agility. They are an intelligent strategy that demonstrates how these animals use every opportunity to gather crucial information. This once again highlights their adaptability and ability to fully exploit their environment to ensure their survival and success in the vast oceans they inhabit.

Fact 26 - Dolphins can synchronize their movements

Dolphins possess a remarkable ability to synchronize their movements, a skill that testifies to their social intelligence and collective coordination. This synchronization, often observed during group hunting or social behavior, enables dolphins to work together extremely efficiently. Whether circling a school of fish or performing synchronized jumps, this ability to harmonize their actions is a distinctive trait that reinforces cohesion and cooperation within the group.

When dolphins hunt in groups, they use this synchronization to maximize their success. For example, by swimming side by side and moving their bodies in perfect alignment, they create pressure waves that force the fish into groups, making them easier to catch. This strategy, which requires precise communication and coordination, shows just how capable dolphins are of working together to achieve a common goal.

This synchronized behavior is also visible in their social interactions, where dolphins often perform jumps or dives in perfect harmony. These synchronized movements are not only a demonstration of their agility, but also a means of strengthening the social bonds between group members. By imitating each other's movements, dolphins reinforce their sense of belonging to the group, and demonstrate their coordination and solidarity.

Scientists have observed that this ability to synchronize movements is learned from an early age. Young dolphins spend a great deal of time observing and imitating the movements of adults, learning to integrate harmoniously into group activities. This learning phase is essential for their social development and future success in group activities.

Synchronized movement in dolphins is much more than a simple demonstration of agility. It is a key element of their survival strategy, illustrating their ability to cooperate, communicate and function as a cohesive unit. This skill is another example of the collective intelligence of dolphins, who know how to exploit their environment and work together to overcome the challenges of life in the ocean.

Fact 27 - Dolphins' hearts beat slowly underwater

As marine mammals, dolphins have developed remarkable adaptations to survive in an aquatic environment. One of the most fascinating is their ability to dramatically slow their heart rate when diving to depth. This phenomenon, known as bradycardia, enables dolphins to conserve oxygen while exploring the ocean depths, prolonging their ability to remain submerged without breathing for several minutes.

When dolphins dive, their bodies go into energy-saving mode. Slowing down the heart is a crucial mechanism in this process. By reducing their heart rate, dolphins limit oxygen consumption, directing blood flow primarily to vital organs such as the brain and heart. This adaptation is essential to enable dolphins to hunt at depths where oxygen is scarce, but prey is abundant.

Studies carried out on diving dolphins have shown that their heart rate can drop dramatically, from 100 beats per minute on the surface to just 20-30 beats per minute when submerged. This slowing of the heart rate is not uniform; it can vary according to depth, dive duration and even the dolphin's physical activity. This flexibility enables dolphins to adapt quickly to changing conditions in their underwater environment.

The effectiveness of this mechanism is particularly impressive in dolphins, which dive to hunt fish or squid at depths of up to several hundred meters. By maintaining a low heart rate, they can prolong their dives while minimizing the risk of oxygen deprivation. This adaptation is a perfect example of the evolutionary ingenuity that enables dolphins to thrive in a variety of environments, from shallow coastal waters to ocean abysses.

The slowing of the heart during diving is a testament to dolphins' ability to master their physiology to survive in extreme conditions. This adaptation gives them great flexibility in their marine lifestyle, enabling them to hunt efficiently and survive in habitats where few other mammals would venture. This complex mechanism is an integral part of what makes dolphins so well adapted to ocean life.

Fact 28 - Dolphins can imitate human sounds

Dolphins have an exceptional ability to imitate the sounds they hear, including those produced by humans. This astonishing ability is a reflection of their vocal intelligence and communication flexibility. Dolphins, particularly bottlenose dolphins (Tursiops truncatus), have been observed imitating whistles, clicks and even sounds produced by mechanical devices, but what is most surprising is their ability to reproduce certain human sounds.

One of the first discoveries of this ability came in the 1960s, when researchers working with captive dolphins found that these animals could imitate simple words or short phrases after hearing them from their trainers. Although dolphins don't understand the meaning of these words, their ability to reproduce sounds with astonishing accuracy shows great mastery of their vocal system. For example, dolphins have been recorded imitating their trainers' names or specific vocal commands.

This imitation of human sounds is not just play or exercise for the dolphins; it also appears to be a form of exploration and learning. Scientists believe that this ability to imitate is an integral part of dolphins' social development, enabling them to strengthen bonds with other dolphins or even with humans. This behavior also demonstrates dolphins' innate curiosity and desire to understand and interact with their environment.

A famous example of this imitation is that of a dolphin named "Aker", who was observed reproducing the sound of a boat engine after hearing it several times. This example shows not only dolphins' ability to imitate, but also their interest in unusual sounds in their environment. It highlights their ability to experiment with the sounds they hear, seeking to understand and reproduce them.

Dolphins' ability to imitate human sounds and other noises is a testament to their vocal intelligence and social nature. This unique talent enables them to explore their world in a very different way to other marine animals, using sounds to bond, communicate and have fun. It's another fascinating aspect of what makes dolphins so incredibly adaptable and interesting.

Fact 29 - Dolphins exchange gifts with each other

Dolphins, known for their intelligence and sociability, have a fascinating behavior: they exchange gifts with each other. This act, which may seem surprisingly human, is actually a way for dolphins to strengthen their social bonds and show affection or respect for another member of the group. The gifts they exchange are not precious objects, but often elements of their environment, such as pieces of seaweed, shells or fish they catch.

This behavior has been observed in various dolphin populations around the world, showing that it is a common trait of the species. For example, in Florida waters, dolphins have been seen to present fish to each other, not for feeding, but as a symbolic act. In some cases, these exchanges take place as part of a game, where the dolphins pass an object from mouth to mouth, throwing and catching it, rather like a ball game.

Gift-giving in dolphins is more than just a playful interaction. It can also have a deeper meaning, particularly in courtship relationships. Males sometimes offer "gifts" to females to attract their attention or to demonstrate their strength and suitability as potential mates. This behavior shows that dolphins use these exchanges not only to play, but also to communicate complex social intentions.

A particularly interesting example of this gift exchange has been documented in bottlenose dolphins, which have been observed offering marine sponges to their fellow dolphins. These sponges, which dolphins sometimes use as tools to protect their rostra when searching the seabed, are also used in these exchanges, showing a form of recognition of the other individual's needs or preferences.

The exchange of gifts between dolphins is further proof of their social complexity and their ability to maintain rich and varied relationships with members of their group. These interactions, far from being trivial, are essential elements of their social life, enabling dolphins to strengthen their bonds, show affection and build lasting alliances. This fascinating behavior underlines once again the emotional intelligence of dolphins and their ability to express feelings in a way that few other animals are able to do.

Fact 30 - Dolphins use echolocation to hunt

Dolphins have a remarkable navigation and hunting system: echolocation. This ability enables them to "see" with sound, by emitting high-frequency clicks that propagate through the water. When these sounds encounter an object, they bounce back to the dolphin as echoes. By analyzing these echoes, the dolphin can determine the size, shape, distance and even texture of the object, be it prey or an obstacle.

Echolocation is particularly useful for dolphins when hunting in low-visibility environments, such as murky or deep waters. Using this technique, they can spot fish hidden in the sand, navigate around coral reefs, or avoid fishing nets. Dolphins emit their clicks in rapid sequences, and the precision of their echolocation is so fine that they can distinguish between different species of fish, or detect an individual fish in a dense school.

This ability to "see" by sound is not only used for hunting. Dolphins also use it to move safely around their environment, particularly at night or in dark waters. By combining echolocation with their exceptional vision and hearing, dolphins are able to create a detailed three-dimensional image of their environment, much like sonar, enabling them to interact effectively with their underwater world.

Echolocation is so sophisticated that it enables dolphins to judge the exact distance of an object by measuring the time it takes for the sound to return to them. The faster the echo returns, the closer the object. Dolphins continually adjust the frequency and intensity of their clicks according to the situation, demonstrating a complex mastery of this natural tool. For example, as they get closer to their prey, clicks become faster and more concentrated, helping them to fine-tune their aim before capturing their meal.

This natural gift for echolocation makes dolphins among the most efficient hunters in the ocean. Their ability to use sound to understand and interact with their environment is further proof of their advanced intelligence and exceptional adaptation to marine life. Thanks to echolocation, dolphins can hunt with precision and navigate with an ease that few other marine animals possess, distinguishing them as one of the ocean's most evolved species.

Fact 31 - Dolphins are the fastest of all cetaceans

Among all cetaceans, dolphins stand out for their incredible speed, making them the sprinters of the ocean. Thanks to their hydrodynamic bodies and powerful musculature, some dolphins, like the short-beaked common dolphin, can reach impressive speeds of up to 60 km/hr. This speed not only enables them to hunt efficiently, but also to evade predators such as sharks.

This blistering speed is the result of several evolutionary adaptations. Their slender bodies reduce water resistance, while their pectoral fins are perfectly designed for fast, precise manoeuvres. Their tail, called the caudal fin, is particularly powerful and plays an essential role in providing efficient propulsion during sprints. These characteristics make dolphins formidable hunters, capable of pursuing and capturing fast-moving prey such as flying fish or mackerel.

In addition to their speed, dolphins are also capable of maintaining remarkable endurance, enabling them to cover long distances in a short time. They often use this ability to migrate to waters richer in food or warmer in winter. Schools of dolphins can travel together over vast stretches of ocean, synchronizing their movements to make the most of their collective speed. This combination of speed and endurance is unique among cetaceans, underlining dolphins' adaptability to diverse marine environments.

Dolphins also use their speed to interact playfully with their environment. It's not uncommon to see them surfing the waves created by boats or jumping out of the water at high speed, demonstrating their agility and enjoyment of play. These behaviors are not only a spectacle for human observers, but also an expression of the dolphins' energetic and social nature.

Their status as the fastest cetaceans is not only an asset to their survival, but also a fascinating trait that continues to captivate researchers and marine life enthusiasts alike. Dolphin speed embodies the power and efficiency with which these animals navigate their vast ocean environment, distinguishing them as the ultimate athletes of the seas.

Fact 32 - Dolphins can detect magnetic fields

Dolphins possess a surprising ability that sets them apart from other marine creatures: they can detect the Earth's magnetic fields. This sense, known as magnetoreception, enables them to orient themselves in the ocean, even in conditions where other landmarks are absent, such as during long-distance migrations or in deep, murky waters. Magnetic fields act as a kind of natural compass, guiding dolphins through their vast marine environment.

Studies have shown that dolphins react differently when exposed to artificial magnetic fields. These observations suggest that dolphins, like certain other animal species, are capable of perceiving variations in the Earth's magnetic fields. This sense could be used for navigation, helping them to locate specific areas they regularly visit, such as hunting or breeding grounds.

This ability is particularly useful for dolphins living in habitats where visual cues are limited, such as deep waters or polar regions. By detecting magnetic fields, dolphins can maintain a precise course even when other sensory cues, such as sight or hearing, are compromised. This enables them to move efficiently and stay in groups, even over long distances.

It is also possible that this ability to detect magnetic fields is used during social interactions or hunting behavior. For example, dolphins could use this ability to detect variations in the environment, which could signal the presence of potential prey or danger. Although research into dolphin magnetoreception is still in its infancy, it is clear that this ability adds a fascinating dimension to their sensory repertoire.

The fact that dolphins can detect magnetic fields shows once again how well adapted these animals are to their environment. This ability, which enables them to navigate and survive in the vastness of the ocean, is a testament to the evolution and sensory complexity of these marine creatures. Dolphins, with their magnetoreception, continue to amaze us with the diverse ways in which they interact with the world around them.

Fact 33 - Dolphins help to care for other dolphins

Dolphins are not only social creatures, but also profoundly altruistic, capable of providing care to their injured or sick fellow creatures. This behavior, observed in many dolphin populations around the world, reveals an empathic dimension to their intelligence, where the needs of other group members are taken into account and addressed. This care goes far beyond simple gestures, sometimes involving concerted efforts to physically support a dolphin in distress.

For example, when one member of a group of dolphins is injured or too weak to swim, the other dolphins support him at the surface, helping him to breathe. This type of intervention has been documented on several occasions, showing that dolphins understand the vital importance of breathing for an individual in difficulty. They then act to prevent drowning, sometimes for hours or even days, until the injured dolphin recovers or the group is forced to leave.

Dolphins also help members of their pod by cleaning their wounds. By rubbing their bodies against those of the injured dolphin, they can help remove parasites or debris that could become infected. Dolphins have been observed rubbing against sand or rocks to clean their own wounds, and they apply this knowledge to help others. This caring and cleaning behavior shows not only an understanding of bodily needs, but also a willingness to actively help another individual.

Another fascinating aspect of this behavior is the social and emotional encouragement dolphins give to their sick or stressed fellow dolphins. They stay close, make soothing sounds, and even rub against the sick dolphin to offer comfort. This physical and vocal interaction demonstrates a form of emotional support, where the dolphins seem to understand and respond to their companions' signs of distress.

This altruistic behavior among dolphins underlines the importance of social bonds within their group. They don't just live together; they actively support each other, creating a community where each member is ready to intervene for the well-being of the others. This ability to care and empathize is an extraordinary aspect of dolphin intelligence, placing them among the most socially complex and compassionate species in the animal kingdom.

Fact 34 - Dolphins surf the waves for fun

Dolphins are known for their playful behavior, and one of their favorite activities is surfing the waves. Unlike many other animal actions motivated by survival or the search for food, dolphin surfing seems to be primarily motivated by pleasure. These intelligent animals use the ocean's natural waves, as well as those generated by boats, to glide gracefully through the water, demonstrating their agility and joie de vivre.

When conditions are ideal, dolphins can be seen gathering near the shore, where they wait for the perfect waves to start their surf. They swim rapidly towards the wave, placing themselves in the right position to be carried away by the water's movement. Once on the crest of the wave, they adjust their posture to maintain balance and prolong their glide as much as possible. This behavior is often accompanied by jumps and spins, demonstrating total mastery of their aquatic environment.

Researchers believe that this surfing behavior is an expression of the social and inquisitive nature of dolphins. They surf not only for themselves, but also in groups, sharing the experience with their companions. This collective activity strengthens social bonds within the group and provides an opportunity for play that is essential to the dolphins' well-being. Surfing thus becomes a form of non-verbal communication, where the dolphins show their energy, vitality and enthusiasm.

Interestingly, this behavior is not limited to natural waves. Dolphins have also been observed surfing on waves created by boats, using the energy of these artificial waves for fun. They often follow boats over long distances, taking every opportunity to jump, dive and turn in the waves. This interaction with man-made elements demonstrates the dolphins' ability to adapt and find pleasure in modified environments.

The fact that dolphins surf the waves simply for fun is a testament to their intelligence and playful nature. This fascinating behavior shows that, like humans, dolphins seek ways to enrich their daily lives with activities that go beyond the needs of survival. For dolphins, surfing is a way of celebrating their freedom, agility and deep connection with the ocean.

Fact 35 - Dolphins have very sensitive skin

Dolphin skin is one of the most sensitive in the animal kingdom, far more delicate than that of many other marine mammals. This skin, although smooth and often described as rubbery, is in fact extremely thin and vulnerable to injury. It is covered by a thin layer of epidermis that renews itself rapidly, almost every two hours, enabling dolphins to maintain a healthy body surface that is efficient for high-speed swimming.

The sensitivity of dolphin skin is largely due to the numerous nerve endings that run through it. These nerve endings make dolphins highly reactive to the slightest touch, whether from other dolphins, objects in their environment, or water currents. This sensitivity enables them to quickly detect changes in their immediate environment, contributing to their ability to avoid predators and interact with their group.

However, this sensitive skin is also a weakness, as it is prone to injuries caused by collisions with rocks, coral, or human equipment such as fishing nets. The scars left by these injuries are often visible on dolphins, but thanks to their rapidly regenerating skin, they can heal without too many complications. Despite this, deep wounds or infections can pose serious health problems.

Dolphins also use their sensitive skin for social interaction. When they rub against each other, they're not just marking their territory or showing dominance; they're also strengthening the social bonds within the group. This gentle rubbing is often a sign of affection and plays an important role in forming and maintaining the complex social relationships between members of a dolphin group.

This extremely sensitive skin, although it has certain disadvantages, is a crucial element in the lives of dolphins. It enables them to stay in close and immediate contact with their environment, to form close social relationships, and to adapt quickly to changes around them. As a barrier between them and the outside world, dolphin skin is a marvel of adaptation, both robust and delicate, enabling them to survive and thrive in the oceans.

Fact 36 - Male dolphins sing to attract females

Dolphins are renowned for their vast repertoire of sounds, and among these vocalizations, male songs play a crucial role in seducing females. These aquatic melodies are emitted during the mating season, serving to signal the male's availability and demonstrate his vitality. These complex songs are an essential part of the mating rituals of many dolphin species.

These vocalizations consist of whistles, clicks and pulses, forming sound patterns unique to each individual. Males modulate the frequency, duration and intensity of their songs to distinguish themselves from their competitors. For example, a healthy male may produce longer, more varied whistles, which could be perceived by females as a sign of vigor and superior genetics.

In bottlenose dolphins, it has been observed that males sometimes form alliances to sing in chorus, creating an underwater symphony designed to attract the attention of females. This cooperative behavior increases their chances of reproductive success, showing that dolphin music is not just an individual act, but can also be a collective strategy.

In a study conducted in the warm waters of the Bahamas, researchers recorded the elaborate songs of male dolphins during the breeding season. These recordings revealed an astonishing richness of sound, with subtle variations in patterns and tones. Females, attracted by these melodies, often approached the singing males, initiating interactions that could lead to mating.

The ability of male dolphins to sing to attract females underlines the importance of acoustic communication in their social and reproductive lives. These songs, a reflection of their intelligence and sensitivity, play a key role in the formation of bonds and the perpetuation of the species. They illustrate the complexity of dolphin interactions and the richness of their underwater sound world.

Fact 37 - Dolphins can communicate with whales

Dolphins have an exceptional capacity for communication that is not limited to their own species. Observations have shown that dolphins can also interact vocally with whales, a fascinating ability that highlights their intelligence and adaptability in the marine world. This inter-species communication occurs mainly during occasional encounters at sea, where the two species exchange vocalizations, sharing their space and sometimes even their activities.

Dolphins use a variety of sounds, including whistles, clicks and calls, to interact with each other, but they also adapt these sounds when in the presence of whales. Bottlenose dolphins, for example, have been observed swimming with humpback whales, modifying their vocalizations to imitate or respond to the whales' songs. These interactions demonstrate a degree of vocal flexibility and understanding between these two species, which differ enormously in size and lifestyle.

In encounters with pilot whales, dolphins have also been seen forming mixed groups, where the two species appear to communicate and coordinate their movements. This collaboration is sometimes linked to hunting, where dolphins and pilot whales share a strategy to capture prey more efficiently. At such times, dolphin vocalizations seem to play a key role in coordinating efforts, reinforcing cooperation between the species.

A striking example of this inter-species communication was observed in the North Atlantic, where dolphins were seen playing around blue whales, emitting complex sounds in response to the calls of these giants of the seas. Although scientists do not yet fully understand the significance of these vocal interactions, it is clear that dolphins are capable of adapting to different social environments and forming temporary bonds with other cetaceans.

This ability of dolphins to communicate with whales reveals not only their cognitive flexibility, but also the richness of social interactions in the marine world. It shows that dolphins are highly social animals, capable of transcending species barriers to interact and cooperate with other cetaceans. This fascinating behavior underlines once again the complexity of the relationships dolphins maintain with their environment and other ocean inhabitants.

Fact 38 - Dolphins rub each other to strengthen their bonds

Dolphins are extremely social animals, and one of the ways they strengthen the bonds within their group is by rubbing against each other. This seemingly innocuous behavior plays a crucial role in maintaining social cohesion among dolphins. When they rub against each other, they're not just sharing a moment of physical closeness; they're also communicating messages of affection, comfort, or reconciliation after a conflict.

Rubbing between dolphins can take many forms, ranging from light contact to more pronounced pressure, often using flippers or the whole body. This behavior is particularly observed between mothers and offspring, where it serves to reinforce the parental bond, but also between adults, where it can be a sign of solidarity or friendship. In a group of dolphins, these tactile exchanges are frequent and essential to maintaining a harmonious, close-knit atmosphere.

Studies have shown that dolphins that regularly rub up against each other develop stronger, longer-lasting social bonds. This behavior is often combined with other positive interactions, such as play or synchronized swimming, further strengthening relationships within the group. Dolphins may also use rubbing to ease tensions after an argument, demonstrating their ability to resolve conflicts and maintain peace within the group.

A poignant example of this behavior has been observed in bottlenose dolphins, where individuals rub up against each other after being separated for some time. This gesture of reunion helps to re-establish social connections and reaffirm their place within the group. What's more, rubbing can also be used to share olfactory information, further strengthening the bonds between group members.

Dolphin rubbing illustrates the importance of physical contact in their social life. They are not only an expression of physical closeness, but also an essential tool for strengthening relationships, easing tensions and ensuring group cohesion. This behavior shows what socially complex creatures dolphins are, capable of developing and maintaining deep, meaningful relationships through simple yet powerful physical interactions.

Fact 39 - Male dolphins cooperate to attract females

Male dolphins have developed a unique and fascinating seduction strategy: cooperation to attract females. Rather than competing against each other, some males form alliances to increase their chances of reproductive success. These cooperative groups, often made up of two or three individuals, work together to woo a female and convince her to join them. This collaborative behavior is particularly observed in bottlenose dolphins, where these alliances can last for several years, reinforcing their effectiveness in the competition for mates.

The seduction process begins with joint displays of strength and skill. Males swim together in synchrony, performing spectacular acrobatics and jumps, while emitting complex vocalizations to attract the female's attention. This precise coordination shows not only their physical fitness, but also their ability to work as a team, a trait that can be perceived as attractive by females. These demonstrations aim to impress the female by highlighting their cohesion and potential as partners.

These alliances are not just temporary; they can last for years and span several breeding seasons. The males involved in these alliances share custody and seduction of the female, increasing their overall chances of reproductive success. In some cases, these alliances may also repel other males attempting to seduce the same female, ensuring that their group has the upper hand in the competition.

A fascinating example of this cooperation has been observed in the dolphins of Shark Bay in Australia, where males form triple alliances, known as "super-alliances". These complex groups support each other not only to attract females, but also to defend themselves against other rival groups. This sophisticated strategy shows how cooperation can be an evolutionary advantage in the competition for the most precious of resources: reproductive partners.

The cooperation between male dolphins to attract females is an astonishing example of their social intelligence and ability to form lasting alliances. Rather than fighting, these dolphins have understood that there is strength in numbers, even in the quest for reproduction.

Fact 40 - Dolphins can eat up to 15 kg of fish

Dolphins are voracious carnivores, and to maintain their energy and agility, they can consume up to 15 kg of fish a day. This impressive quantity is necessary to support their rapid metabolism, constant activity and sometimes long-distance movements. Dolphins' dietary requirements vary according to their size, species and environment, but one thing is clear: they are formidable hunters in the ocean.

Their diet consists mainly of fish, but they also hunt squid and other small marine creatures. To capture their prey, dolphins use a variety of sophisticated hunting techniques, often in groups. For example, they may encircle a school of fish to group them into a compact mass, thus facilitating their capture. Once they have isolated their prey, dolphins show great skill in using their speed and agility to seize it.

Dolphins don't chew their food like many other animals. They generally swallow their prey whole, their mouths and teeth being perfectly adapted to this mode of feeding. Dolphins' teeth are not used to crush food, but rather to grasp and hold their prey firmly, which they then swallow quickly. This mode of consumption enables them to maximize their food intake in the shortest possible time, which is essential for their survival.

In some cases, dolphins can adjust their consumption according to the availability of food resources. During periods of abundance, they may eat more to build up energy reserves. Conversely, they are also able to survive on less food during periods of scarcity, thanks to their ability to regulate their metabolism. This dietary flexibility is another reason why dolphins are so well adapted to life in varied marine environments.

The fact that dolphins can consume up to 15 kg of fish a day underlines their role as efficient predators in the marine ecosystem. Their diet places them at the top of the food chain, where they play a crucial role in maintaining the balance of fish populations and other marine creatures. This ability to hunt and consume large quantities of food is an essential characteristic that enables them to survive and thrive in the vast oceans.

Fact 41 - Dolphins avoid sharks in groups

Despite their agility and intelligence, dolphins can fall prey to sharks, those fearsome marine predators. However, to protect themselves, dolphins have developed a highly effective collective strategy: they travel in groups. This behavior is an excellent example of their social instinct and their ability to work together to ensure their survival. By forming close-knit groups called schools, dolphins increase their safety and reduce the risk of attack by sharks.

When a dolphin spots a shark, it immediately alerts the other members of the group by emitting specific sounds and displaying agitated behavior. In response, the dolphins quickly regroup, forming a sort of protective barrier around the most vulnerable members, such as the young or injured. This uniting behavior is an instinctive response that makes it more difficult for the shark to target an isolated individual. In groups, dolphins can even go on the offensive, harassing the shark to repel it, a tactic that has often proved effective.

The very structure of the dolphin group plays a crucial role in this defense strategy. Each member of the group knows his or her position and role, and the strongest dolphins often take up positions on the periphery to protect the center of the shoal. This complex social organization enables dolphins to react quickly and in a coordinated fashion to danger, minimizing losses and risks for the group as a whole.

It's also interesting to note that sharks are less likely to attack a group of dolphins than a single individual. The presence of the group often deters the shark, which prefers to avoid a potentially dangerous confrontation. By employing this collective strategy, dolphins exploit not only their numbers, but also their ability to collaborate effectively, which is one of the many aspects that testify to their intelligence.

In short, moving in groups is much more than a simple social habit for dolphins; it's an essential survival tactic in an ocean where predators are numerous. Their ability to avoid sharks by staying together demonstrates the importance of cooperation and communication within their species, and underlines their remarkable adaptation to a sometimes hostile marine environment.

Fact 42 - Dolphins can play with algae

Dolphins, known for their inquisitive and playful nature, often find creative ways to amuse themselves in their marine environment. One such fascinating behavior is their habit of playing with algae. When they come across floating seaweed, dolphins often grab it with their rostrum (snout) and manipulate it with astonishing agility. They throw these pieces of algae at each other, swirl them around in the water, and sometimes even carry them on their heads or backs.

Playing with algae is not only a simple pastime for dolphins, it also strengthens their social bonds. Young dolphins, in particular, often use these games to interact with their peers, learning to navigate their environment and develop motor skills. Playing with algae also enables dolphins to practice behaviors that will serve them well into adulthood, such as object manipulation and movement coordination.

Scientists who have observed this behavior have noted that dolphins can spend long periods playing with algae, showing clear signs of pleasure and excitement. They may also involve other members of their group, transforming this simple game into a collective activity. Dolphins take turns catching and throwing algae, showing remarkable coordination and cooperation.

One of the reasons why dolphins play with seaweed may be its texture and buoyancy. Seaweed is easy to handle and reacts in interesting ways to underwater movements, making it particularly attractive to dolphins. What's more, these games allow the dolphins to explore their environment and stay mentally stimulated, which is crucial for such intelligent and social animals.

By playing with algae, dolphins once again demonstrate their creativity and ability to interact with their environment in complex ways. This behavior underlines the importance of play in the lives of dolphins, not only as a means of entertainment, but also as an essential aspect of their social and cognitive development. By using the natural resources at their disposal to have fun, dolphins show how adaptable and ingenious they are in their daily interactions.

Fact 43 - Dolphins are born with the ability to echolocate

Dolphins come into the world with an extraordinary gift: the ability to use echolocation, a vital skill that enables them to navigate and hunt in the complex aquatic environment. From birth, young dolphins possess the biological structures needed to emit sonar clicks and interpret the resulting echoes. This innate ability is essential to their survival, enabling them to situate themselves in space, avoid obstacles and detect the presence of prey or predators.

At birth, although this ability is present, it is rudimentary and requires some development. Young dolphins spend many hours honing their echolocation skills under the tutelage of their mother and other members of the pod. During this learning period, they frequently emit clicks and sounds, playing with the echoes they receive to better understand their environment. This process of experimentation and refinement continues throughout their growth, making their echolocation increasingly precise and efficient.

Dolphin mothers play a crucial role in this development, guiding their young through different environments and exposing them to various situations that require the use of echolocation. For example, they often take them into deeper or darker waters where vision is limited, encouraging the young to rely more on their sonar ability to navigate and find their way. This collaborative learning process strengthens the bond between mother and offspring, while fostering the latter's future independence.

Dolphins' echolocation is so sophisticated that it enables them to discern incredibly fine details, such as the texture, shape and even density of objects. This precision gives them a distinct advantage when hunting and exploring their habitat. For young dolphins, learning to master this ability means acquiring the skills needed to capture prey, avoid danger, and communicate with other members of their pod.

By being born with the ability to echolocate, dolphins inherit not only a unique sense, but also an essential tool that structures their daily lives. This skill, developed and perfected from the very first days of their lives, is one of the many characteristics that make dolphins such remarkably well-adapted marine creatures.

Fact 44 - Dolphins can travel hundreds of miles

Dolphins are tireless travelers, capable of covering hundreds of kilometers across the oceans. Their incredible endurance and ability to navigate over long distances are due to several natural adaptations, including their hydrodynamic bodies, powerful musculature, and ability to regulate their energy efficiently. This migratory or exploratory behavior enables them to search for food resources, find mates, or move to warmer waters depending on the season.

These long-distance movements are often dictated by the dolphins' feeding needs. By following ocean currents, they can move to areas where fish are more abundant. For example, some dolphin species, such as the short-beaked common dolphin, are known for their seasonal migrations, which take them hundreds of kilometers to reach prey-rich hunting grounds. This behavior enables them to survive in constantly changing marine environments, where resource availability can change rapidly.

Dolphins don't always travel alone; they often travel in groups, or shoals, which can number several dozen individuals. Traveling in groups offers several advantages, including greater protection from predators such as sharks, and better coordination when hunting. Group members communicate with each other using a variety of sounds to coordinate and stay on course during their long journeys. This constant communication is essential to ensure that the whole group stays together and achieves its goal.

A striking example of dolphins' ability to travel long distances is that of bottlenose dolphins, which have been observed traveling distances of over 1,000 kilometers in just a few weeks. These journeys can be influenced by environmental factors, such as water temperatures, weather conditions and the presence of favorable ocean currents. Dolphins are also capable of locating underwater landmarks and orienting themselves using magnetic cues, enabling them to navigate with precision over vast stretches of ocean.

Fact 45 - Dolphins have a special laugh during play

Dolphins are known for their playful behavior and their ability to interact in complex ways with their environment and companions. Among their many vocalizations, researchers have discovered that dolphins produce a peculiar, laughter-like sound when they play. This "laugh" manifests itself as a series of short, rhythmic sounds, often made during social play, such as chasing, synchronized jumping, or playing with objects like seaweed or fish.

This special laugh is more than just a vocalization; it seems to play an important role in the dolphins' social communication. During playful interactions, this sound may serve to indicate to other dolphins that the activity is purely friendly and non-aggressive. In this way, laughter helps to maintain peace and harmony within the group, clarifying each individual's intentions and preventing misunderstandings.

Scientists who have observed this behavior suggest that laughter may also strengthen social bonds between dolphins. By laughing together, dolphins create a shared experience that consolidates their relationship. This phenomenon is similar to that observed in humans, where collective laughter plays a crucial role in creating and maintaining social bonds. The fact that dolphins have a vocalization dedicated to play once again demonstrates their social and emotional sophistication.

This dolphin laughter is most often heard in young individuals, who spend much of their time playing. However, adults also take part in these games and laugh with their fellow dolphins, showing that play and fun are important elements in the lives of dolphins of all ages. Playful moments accompanied by laughter contribute to the dolphins' mental and physical well-being, offering them an escape from the daily challenges of survival at sea.

Dolphins' laughter is further proof of their intelligence and ability to express complex emotions. By observing these behaviors, scientists continue to discover the richness of the dolphin social world and understand how these marine creatures communicate, interact and maintain harmonious relationships within their groups.

Fact 46 - Dolphins have a double layer of skin

Dolphins have a fascinating skin that is structured to help them navigate efficiently in their marine environment. One of the remarkable features of their skin is that it consists of two distinct layers: an outer layer called the epidermis, and an inner layer called the dermis. This double layer plays a crucial role not only in protecting the dolphin, but also in optimizing its aquatic performance.

The outer layer, or epidermis, is surprisingly thick compared to that of other marine mammals. It is smooth, elastic and renews itself rapidly, often every two hours. This ability to renew itself rapidly enables dolphins to minimize damage caused by the marine environment, such as friction with water, superficial wounds, and even the attachment of parasites. What's more, the smooth nature of the epidermis helps reduce water resistance, enabling dolphins to swim faster and more efficiently.

The inner layer, the dermis, is denser and contains collagen fibers, which provide additional structure and strength. The dermis is also rich in blood vessels, which help regulate the dolphin's body temperature, a vital aspect for marine mammals that spend time in waters of different temperatures. In fact, this inner layer acts as an insulator, protecting the dolphin from cold temperatures while maintaining a flexibility that allows it to move with ease.

This double layer of skin not only acts as a protective barrier, but also plays an active role in sensory perception. Dolphins have numerous nerve endings in their skin, particularly in the dermis, which enable them to detect the slightest changes in their environment, such as water movements, the presence of prey, or vibrations emitted by other sea creatures. This tactile sensitivity is essential to their survival, enabling them to react quickly to external stimuli.

Dolphins' double-layered skin system is a marvel of evolutionary adaptation, offering enhanced protection, thermal regulation and sensory capacity. It enables them to thrive in often hostile marine environments, while giving them the advantage of moving quickly and with great precision.

Fact 47 - Dolphins can recognize a lost limb

Dolphins possess an astonishingly well-developed social memory, enabling them to recognize members of their group even after long separations. This remarkable ability is the result of their social intelligence and sophisticated communication skills. When a dolphin finds itself away from its group for any reason, such as foraging or migration, it may be absent for months or even years. However, when they are reunited with their group, they are often greeted with a warm welcome, as if they had never been away.

Scientists have observed that dolphins use their ability to recognize vocal signatures to identify individuals. Each dolphin has a distinctive whistle, comparable to a name, which remains stable throughout its life. Even after years of separation, a dolphin can recognize this particular whistle, enabling it to reunite with a former companion or family member. These reunions often manifest themselves in exchanges of whistles, body rubs and palpable excitement within the group.

A striking example of this ability has been documented in bottlenose dolphins, where an individual had been separated from his group for over ten years. When he was reintroduced, the other dolphins immediately recognized him and resumed their social interaction as if there had never been a separation. This kind of behavior is rare in the animal kingdom and underlines just how social creatures dolphins are, with impressive long-term memories.

This recognition of lost members is crucial to group cohesion, as it helps maintain strong social bonds, even after periods of absence. This is particularly important for species such as dolphins, where cooperation and solidarity within the group are essential for survival, whether hunting or protecting against predators. The ability to remember and recognize an individual after a long absence shows just how much dolphins value relationships within their group.

Fact 48 - Dolphins change partners regularly

Dolphins, unlike some other animal species, do not form permanent pair bonds. Instead, they regularly change partners, a strategy that is an integral part of their complex social life and reproductive behavior. This way of life, where partnerships are often ephemeral, enables dolphins to increase genetic diversity within their population, which is beneficial to the overall health of the species.

Dolphin relationships are characterized by great flexibility and the absence of strict single parenthood. During the mating season, males and females interact freely, with multiple partners. These interactions are not limited to reproduction, but also include social behaviors such as play and cooperation. Alliances between males can even influence mate choice, with some males forming coalitions to court females together.

The practice of regularly changing partners in dolphins is also a way of avoiding inbreeding, a key factor in maintaining genetic diversity. By having several partners during their lifetime, dolphins minimize the risk of transmitting genetic diseases and maximize their offspring's chances of survival. This also ensures greater variability in offspring traits, which can be advantageous in changing marine environments.

Observations in the wild, such as those carried out on bottlenose dolphins in Shark Bay, Australia, have shown that dolphins can have different partners from one season to the next, and even within the same season. These varied relationships are not only focused on reproduction, but also serve to strengthen social networks within groups, with each interaction contributing to the social balance of the dolphin community.

The Fact that dolphins regularly change partners is an illustration of their dynamic and adaptive social behavior. This flexible system enables them not only to maximize their reproductive success, but also to maintain complex, balanced social relationships within their groups. Due to their sociable nature and intelligence, dolphins have developed partnership strategies that ensure not only their survival, but also the health and vitality of their species.

Fact 49 - Dolphins teach their young to hunt

Dolphins are caring and devoted parents, and one of the most crucial responsibilities of dolphin mothers is to teach their young the art of hunting. From an early age, young dolphins begin to observe and imitate the hunting techniques of their mothers and other members of the pod. This learning process is essential to their survival, as it enables them to develop the skills needed to capture the prey that will constitute their main diet throughout their lives.

The process of teaching hunting skills usually begins with simple demonstrations, in which the mother shows her calf how to spot and track fish or squid. The young dolphins also learn to use specific techniques, such as creating bubbles to trap fish or cooperating with other dolphins to surround a school of prey. These lessons are repeated again and again, each session building the young dolphin's confidence and skill in the water.

One of the most fascinating techniques observed in certain dolphin populations is the use of sea sponges as hunting tools. Mothers teach their young how to place a sponge on their rostrum to protect their sensitive skin when searching the seabed for hidden fish. This behavior, transmitted from generation to generation, shows how important social learning is in dolphins, and how they are able to pass on complex cultural knowledge.

The learning process is not just passive; young dolphins are encouraged to try things out for themselves, under their mother's watchful supervision. This hands-on learning method allows the youngsters to develop their own techniques while benefiting from their mother's support and correction. The time spent perfecting these skills varies, but can last several years, with dolphins continuing to hone their skills long after they've been weaned.

Teaching young dolphins to hunt illustrates their ability to learn and transmit complex knowledge, a trait that testifies to their remarkable intelligence. This process of cultural transmission is a key element of dolphin life, enabling future generations to adapt to the changing challenges of their marine environment.

Fact 50 - Dolphins can save humans from drowning

Dolphins have repeatedly been the heroes of incredible stories in which they have saved humans from drowning. This altruistic behavior, observed in different parts of the world, shows the extent to which these marine creatures are capable of reacting to emergency situations with astonishing intelligence and sensitivity. Far from being a simple instinct, these actions testify to a complex understanding of the needs of other living beings, even those of a different species.

Testimonials of people rescued by dolphins are numerous and often share striking similarities. For example, a swimmer in trouble or drowning is often surrounded by a group of dolphins, who support him and push him towards the water's surface or the shore. These behaviors are all the more remarkable in that the dolphins act voluntarily and without any external prompting, as if they understand the gravity of the situation.

Scientists have put forward several hypotheses to explain why dolphins act in this way. Some believe that dolphins recognize signs of distress in humans, as they display similar characteristics to their own young when in trouble. Others suggest that dolphins are naturally curious and socially oriented, prompting them to intervene when they perceive imminent danger. Whatever the exact reason, these rescues continue to fascinate and amaze those who witness them.

One of the most famous stories dates back to 2004, when several swimmers in New Zealand were protected from a shark attack by a pod of dolphins. The dolphins formed a circle around the swimmers, preventing the shark from approaching, and escorted them safely to the beach. The incident attracted international attention and reinforced the reputation of dolphins as guardians of the oceans, always ready to intervene in times of need.

Dolphins' behavior towards humans is a poignant testament to their emotional intelligence and their ability to perceive and react to emergency situations. Although the reasons for these rescues remain partly mysterious, they underline the special bond that can form between dolphins and humans, a bond based on trust, understanding and a shared instinct to preserve life.

Fact 51 - Dolphins prefer warm waters

Dolphins, those graceful marine mammals, are particularly attracted to warm waters. The majority of dolphin species are regularly observed in the tropical and subtropical zones of the world's oceans, where water temperatures are pleasantly warm throughout the year. This preference for warm waters is linked to a number of factors, including the availability of food, ease of navigation and ideal conditions for breeding.

In warmer waters, marine ecosystems are often richer in biodiversity, offering an abundance of fish and squid, which form the basis of dolphins' diet. Coral reefs and tropical coastal areas teem with marine life, attracting dolphins to these areas where they can hunt effectively. Warm waters also facilitate the growth of young dolphins, as higher temperatures contribute to a stable and nourishing environment for newborns.

In addition to the abundance of food, warm waters offer a more comfortable living environment for dolphins. These creatures don't have a thick layer of insulating blubber like whales, and warm waters help maintain their body temperature. Although some dolphins can live in colder waters, the majority prefer regions where the water temperature remains moderate, minimizing the energy required to maintain their body heat.

Reproduction is another factor that drives dolphins to warm waters. In these areas, conditions are often more favorable for the birth and rearing of young. Warm, shallow waters offer shelter from predators and allow mother dolphins to feed and protect their young in complete safety. These environments are also conducive to social interaction, as dolphins often gather in these areas to form schools and interact with other groups.

Dolphins' habitat is therefore closely linked to warm waters, where they find not only an abundant food supply, but also optimal living conditions for survival and reproduction. This preference for warm waters explains why these creatures are often spotted near tropical and subtropical coasts, offering observers the opportunity to admire their beauty and agility in lush, welcoming marine environments.

Fact 52 - Dolphins can live in rivers

Although dolphins are generally associated with the oceans, some species have successfully adapted to life in freshwater, living in rivers. River dolphins, such as the Amazon river dolphin, also known as the boto, and the Ganges river dolphin, have developed specific characteristics that enable them to thrive in these river environments. These dolphins are able to navigate in waters that are often murky and shallow, far removed from the vast expanses of sea that their ocean cousins roam.

River dolphins are distinguished by several unique adaptations. For example, the Amazon river dolphin has a longer beak and smaller eyes than its marine counterparts. These features enable them to efficiently search river bottoms for fish and crustaceans, their main source of food. In addition, their ability to navigate in shallow waters is facilitated by their smaller dorsal fin, which helps them maneuver in environments cluttered with aquatic vegetation and debris.

River dolphin habitats are often rich and complex ecosystems. Rivers such as the Amazon and the Ganges offer a wide diversity of prey and favorable conditions for their survival. However, these environments can also be extremely changeable, with significant seasonal variations in water level. River dolphins are therefore particularly resilient and able to adapt to these changes, surviving periods of drought or flash floods by moving to more suitable sections of the river.

Living in rivers also means facing unique challenges. River dolphins often have to navigate among human activities, such as fishing, shipping and the exploitation of natural resources. Despite these challenges, these dolphins have developed behaviors that enable them to avoid danger and coexist with local communities. For example, some river dolphins are known to follow fishing boats to capture fish escaping from nets, showing remarkable ingenuity.

The fact that some dolphin species have evolved to live in rivers demonstrates their incredible adaptability. These river dolphins offer a fascinating example of the diversity of the cetacean family, thriving in habitats as varied as the vast oceans and the complex meanders of river systems.

Fact 53 - Dolphins have a developed cerebral cortex

Dolphins are often recognized for their exceptional intelligence, and one of the main reasons for this advanced cognitive ability lies in their highly developed cerebral cortex. The cerebral cortex is the part of the brain responsible for higher functions such as thinking, perception, memory and decision-making. In dolphins, this region is particularly large and complex, compared to that of many other animals, including some primates.

The cerebral cortex of dolphins features numerous convolutions, folds and hollows that increase the surface area of the brain without increasing its volume. This feature is often associated with higher cognitive abilities, as it enables more sophisticated information processing. Dolphins use their developed cerebral cortex to perform a variety of complex tasks, such as whistle communication, problem solving, and even self-recognition in a mirror.

Research has shown that the cerebral cortex of dolphins is not only large, but also densely populated with neurons, the nerve cells that transmit information. This neuronal density contributes to their capacity for rapid learning and long-term memory. For example, dolphins are able to retain and reproduce sequences of whistles or movements long after they have learned them, demonstrating a sophisticated memory and ability to imitate complex behaviors.

Another crucial function of the cerebral cortex is the management of emotions and social interactions. In dolphins, this region is involved in the formation of deep social bonds, cooperation within groups, and empathy towards fellow creatures. These animals are able to understand the intentions of others, form strategic alliances, and even demonstrate altruistic behaviors, such as helping injured members of their group.

The advanced development of the cerebral cortex in dolphins underlines their position as one of the most intelligent creatures on the planet. This sophisticated brain enables them not only to survive in complex environments, but also to thrive socially and cognitively. Studies of the dolphin brain continue to reveal fascinating insights into the nature of animal intelligence, offering valuable glimpses into how these incredible marine mammals perceive and interact with the world around them.

Fact 54 - Dolphins can feel the pain of others

Dolphins are deeply empathetic creatures, capable of feeling the pain and distress of other individuals, whether fellow dolphins or even other species. This empathic behavior, which is often observed in situations where a member of the group is injured or in difficulty, shows just how socially and emotionally connected these animals are to each other. Their ability to perceive and react to the suffering of others is a sign of their advanced emotional intelligence.

Observations in the wild have revealed that when one member of a group of dolphins is injured, the other members of the group often gather around him. They will support him physically, for example by holding him at the water's surface to help him breathe, or by emitting specific sounds, such as whistles and clicks, which appear to be calls or signals of comfort. These behaviors are not simply automatic; they show an awareness of the situation and a willingness to help a fellow animal in distress.

Dolphins don't reserve their empathy for their own species alone. There are stories of dolphins coming to the aid of other marine animals, and even humans, in danger. For example, there are documented cases of dolphins protecting swimmers from shark attacks or guiding boats to individuals in distress. These altruistic acts suggest that dolphins can perceive the distress of other living beings and are ready to intervene to help them, even at the risk of their own safety.

Dolphin empathy is also observed in the relationship between mothers and offspring. Dolphin mothers show particular attention to their newborns, responding quickly to signs of pain or distress. They comfort them by gently touching them with their flippers or holding them close. This protective behavior often extends beyond the dependency period, showing that social and emotional bonds in dolphins are long-lasting and deeply rooted.

This level of compassion and understanding of others' pain distinguishes dolphins as one of the most socially sophisticated species in the ocean. Their ability to feel the pain of others, combined with their intelligence and communication skills, makes them particularly remarkable in the animal kingdom.

Fact 55 - Dolphins have a sense of humor

Dolphins are more than just intelligent marine creatures; they also possess a sense of humor, a trait that makes them even more fascinating. This sense of humor often manifests itself in playful behavior and social interactions, where they seem to enjoy playing pranks or games with other dolphins, and even with humans. Their ability to engage in play and enjoy amusing situations demonstrates a joyful, mischievous side rarely seen in the animal kingdom.

A striking example of this sense of humor is the playful behavior of dolphins when interacting with objects or other animals. They have been known to play with seaweed, fish or even bubbles, tossing them in the air or passing them from one dolphin to another. Sometimes, they seem to play tricks on their fellow dolphins by hiding objects or gently teasing them with their fins. These games are not simply ways of passing the time; they show that the dolphins find pleasure in these interactions and repeat them voluntarily to amuse themselves.

Dolphins also interact with humans in ways that reflect their sense of humor. In some cases, they imitate the movements of swimmers or divers, seeming to participate in a mirror game. It's not uncommon for a dolphin to splash a swimmer on purpose, as if to provoke an amused reaction. These behaviors are not mere coincidences, but show that dolphins actively seek to create moments of shared fun.

The scientists observed that these moments of humor and play are often accompanied by specific vocalizations, such as whistles or clicks, which seem to correspond to laughter. Although these sounds are different from human laughter, they seem to play a similar role in communication and strengthening social bonds between dolphins. These joyful vocalizations are often heard during the most animated social interactions, reinforcing the idea that dolphins find real pleasure in play and jokes.

Dolphins' sense of humor is further proof of their intelligence and emotional complexity. It shows that, like humans, they are capable of feeling pleasure and seeking out positive experiences, not only for their survival, but also for their social well-being.

Fact 56 - Dolphins make different sounds in different situations

Dolphins are masters of underwater communication, using an impressive variety of sounds to interact with their environment and fellow dolphins. Each situation seems to call for a specific type of sound, demonstrating the breadth of their vocal repertoire and the sophistication of their language. The researchers identified several types of vocalizations, including whistles, clicks and squeaks, each associated with a particular behavior or need.

Whistling, for example, is often used for identification and recognition between dolphins. Each individual has a unique signature whistle, comparable to a name, which it emits to signal its presence to others. When a dolphin moves away from the group, it may emit this whistle to maintain contact with its fellow dolphins. This ability to use specific whistles enables dolphins to remain in constant communication, even at great distances or in murky waters.

Clicks, meanwhile, play a crucial role in echolocation, a natural sonar system that dolphins use to move, hunt and explore their environment. By emitting clicks and analyzing the returning echoes, a dolphin can determine the distance, size, shape and texture of an object or prey. These sounds are shorter and sharper than whistles, suited to the precise task of navigating and hunting in the darkness of the deep sea.

In situations of stress or conflict, dolphins may emit grunts or growls, which are rougher, more intense sounds. These vocalizations are often associated with defensive or aggressive behavior, and serve to deter rivals or express a form of irritation. For example, when competing for food or a mate, dolphins use these sounds to establish hierarchies or signal dominance.

Dolphins' ability to make different sounds in different situations illustrates not only their intelligence, but also the depth of their social interactions. Their rich and varied language is an essential tool for navigating their underwater world, where communication plays a central role in their survival and well-being. Studies on these vocalizations continue to offer fascinating insights into how dolphins perceive and interact with their environment, enhancing our understanding of these amazing creatures.

Fact 57 - Dolphins have complex social relationships

Dolphins are renowned for their complex social relationships, which rival those of many animal species, including humans. They live in groups called shoals, which can vary in size from a few individuals to dozens or even hundreds, depending on the circumstances. These groups are not just random gatherings; they are structured around deep, dynamic social relationships, where individuals form alliances, friendships and hierarchies.

Relationships between dolphins are marked by intense cooperation. For example, males may form small teams to attract and protect females, working together to maximize their chances of reproductive success. These alliances can last for many years, demonstrating a level of cooperation and trust rare in the animal kingdom. What's more, these relationships are not static; they can evolve over time, with dolphins changing partners or groups according to need and opportunity.

Females, for their part, also maintain strong social relationships, often centered around motherhood and raising their young. They form sub-groups to help each other, exchange information and protect their young. This mutual support is crucial to the survival of newborns, who depend heavily on their mother and other group members to learn to hunt, protect themselves from predators and navigate their complex environment.

Social relationships in dolphins are not limited to interactions within the same group. Sometimes, different shoals meet and interact peacefully, sometimes even playing together or temporarily exchanging members. This ability to interact with outside groups demonstrates an impressive social flexibility, enabling dolphins to adapt to varied environments and maintain a rich and varied social dynamic.

Dolphins' social behaviors also include gestures of affection, such as rubbing against each other or swimming in synchrony. These interactions strengthen bonds within the group and play a key role in social cohesion. The complexity of these relationships demonstrates that dolphins are not only intelligent creatures, but also deeply social, capable of forming lasting and meaningful bonds with their fellow creatures.

Fact 58 - Dolphins can blow air rings

Dolphins are capable of a fascinating feat that testifies to their intelligence and skill: they can blow rings of air underwater. These rings, also known as "ring-shaped air bubbles", are created by blowing a jet of air through their blowhole, then manipulating it with precise head and body movements. These air rings are surprisingly stable and can last for several seconds, floating in the water like perfect circles.

Blowing air rings seems to be a playful activity for dolphins. They create these bubbles not out of necessity, but for pleasure, demonstrating once again their ability to play and experiment with their environment. After blowing a ring, they can have fun pushing it, spinning it or even crossing it with their bodies, demonstrating remarkable coordination and precision. This behavior reveals a creative and mischievous side of their personality.

Scientists believe that this ability to blow air rings may also have a social dimension. Dolphins are highly social animals, and they may use these rings as a means of interacting with each other, strengthening bonds within the group. It's not uncommon to see several dolphins playing with the rings together, passing them from one individual to another or observing them with shared curiosity.

From a physical point of view, creating these air rings requires a detailed understanding of aquatic dynamics. Dolphins must precisely control how much air they blow and how they direct it to create a perfect ring. This manipulation demonstrates not only their intelligence, but also their ability to master the elements of their environment with surprising skill.

By blowing these rings of air, dolphins once again illustrate their cognitive complexity and propensity for fun. These ephemeral, elegant air bubbles are not only a fascinating sight to observe, but also a demonstration of dolphins' ability to interact with their environment in ways that go beyond simple survival needs. This behavior adds to the long list of incredible talents that make dolphins one of our planet's most remarkable species.

Fact 59 - Dolphins explore new territories in groups

Dolphins are curious and organized explorers when it comes to discovering new territories. Rather than venturing out on their own, they prefer to do so in groups, which not only enables them to share discoveries, but also to protect each other. This collective exploration is an essential strategy for adapting to changing environments and finding new food sources or resting places.

When dolphins decide to explore a new area, they use their collective intelligence to assess risks and opportunities. For example, they may send a few scouts ahead, while the rest of the group waits at a safe distance. These scouts use their echolocation to map the new space, detect the presence of predators or obstacles, and locate resources such as schools of fish. Once the information has been gathered, they return to the group to share their findings, enabling everyone to make an informed decision about the next step in the exploration.

This group exploration is not limited to the search for food. Dolphins have also been known to venture into new territories simply out of curiosity. For example, they may be attracted by unusual noises, unfamiliar underwater structures, or even other marine species they don't often have the opportunity to encounter. These forays into unexplored territories enable dolphins to enrich their experience of the world and maintain an active social dynamic.

Cooperation between group members during these explorations is paramount. Each dolphin has a role to play, whether it's protecting the young, keeping an eye on the surroundings, or leading the advance. This complex social organization is a major asset to their survival, enabling them to cope with the unexpected and adapt quickly to new situations. What's more, exploring in a group strengthens the bonds between dolphins, as they share the excitement of discovery and the challenges encountered along the way.

These group explorations of new territories illustrate the ability of dolphins to work together harmoniously and efficiently. Their natural curiosity and ability to collaborate enable them to navigate successfully in diverse and sometimes hostile environments. Relying on their collective intelligence, dolphins continue to discover and exploit the riches of their underwater world, demonstrating once again their adaptability and exceptional team spirit.

Fact 60 - Dolphins communicate by coding their sounds

Dolphins have an extraordinarily complex communication system based on the emission of a variety of sounds, which they code to convey specific messages. These sounds include whistles, clicks and squeaks, each with a specific meaning. This sound coding enables dolphins to express a wide variety of information, such as their identity, their emotional state, or indications of their immediate environment.

Scientists have discovered that dolphins can modulate the frequency, intensity and duration of these sounds to form "words" or "phrases" in their own language. For example, a single whistle can be used as a "name" to identify a particular dolphin, while a series of rapid clicks can be used to signal the presence of food. This ability to structure sounds in such an elaborate way demonstrates an advanced cognitive intelligence, comparable to that of great apes and even humans.

This coded language is also crucial for coordinating actions within a group. When hunting or exploring, dolphins use their coded sounds to synchronize their movements and share important information. For example, they may alert other dolphins to the presence of predators, or guide a group member to a food source. This sophisticated communication is essential to their survival, enabling them to function as a coherent unit in an often unpredictable environment.

Dolphins' coded sounds are not only functional, they also play a social role. Dolphins "converse" with each other to strengthen bonds, share experiences or simply play. It's common to hear them emit rhythmic or repeated sounds during social interactions, as if they were "talking" to each other. These vocal exchanges are often accompanied by physical behaviors, such as jumping or rubbing, which further enrich their communication.

By encoding their sounds, dolphins demonstrate a rare ability among animals: that of creating a flexible, adaptable language capable of expressing complex concepts. This advanced communication system enables them to navigate their environment with remarkable efficiency, while maintaining close social relationships.

Fact 61 - Dolphins can swim backwards

Dolphins are renowned for their aquatic prowess, and among their surprising talents is the ability to swim backwards. This uncommon skill among marine mammals is a testament to their exceptional agility and body control. Unlike swimming forwards, where propulsion is provided by the dolphin's powerful tail, swimming backwards requires precise coordination between several body parts.

Dolphins mainly use their pectoral fins to move backwards. By rapidly flapping these fins and subtly altering the angle of their bodies, they propel themselves in the opposite direction. This movement is often observed during complex maneuvers, for example when exploring narrow areas or interacting with objects or conspecifics. This ability to swim backwards enables them to demonstrate great flexibility in their movements.

This inverted swimming pattern is also useful in social interactions between dolphins. Sometimes they use it to gently withdraw from a situation without turning their backs on their fellow dolphins, which can be interpreted as a sign of respect or courtesy in their complex social relationships. This skill adds an extra dimension to the finesse with which dolphins communicate and interact with each other.

The ability to swim backwards is also an asset for survival. When a dolphin is faced with a potentially dangerous situation, such as an encounter with a predator, being able to retreat quickly while keeping an eye on the threat can be crucial. This enables it to react swiftly in the event of an attack, while preparing itself for a possible escape move.

This skill perfectly illustrates the adaptability and intelligence of dolphins. Their mastery of various swimming techniques, including backwards, enables them to navigate their complex environment efficiently, ensure their own safety, and maintain harmonious social relationships. This underlines once again what remarkably sophisticated creatures dolphins are, and how well adapted they are to marine life.

Fact 62 - Dolphins help other species in distress

Dolphins don't just help members of their own species; they have also been known to come to the aid of other animals in distress. This altruistic behavior is particularly impressive, and underlines their emotional intelligence and capacity for compassion. Numerous sightings report cases of dolphins coming to the aid of beached whales, sea turtles in trouble or even fish trapped in nets.

For example, there are accounts of dolphins surrounding a stranded whale in an attempt to guide it to deeper water. These inter-species interactions show that dolphins are capable of recognizing the distress of another animal and reacting to help it. This type of behavior is rare in the animal kingdom, especially between different species, which makes dolphins all the more fascinating.

Dolphins have also been observed protecting other animals from predator attacks. For example, dolphins have been seen forming a protective barrier around a seal to defend it from sharks. This ability to risk their own safety to protect another living being is a striking testament to their moral and social sense, a trait rarely seen with such complexity in other animals.

Their ability to collaborate and show empathy for other species reflects a high level of social awareness. It is possible that this instinctive mutual aid is the fruit of their complex social life, where cooperation and communication are essential to survival. By helping other animals, dolphins demonstrate their ability to extend these skills beyond their own species.

This altruistic behavior in dolphins is much admired by researchers, and reinforces the idea that these cetaceans possess advanced social intelligence. The study of these interactions could even offer insights into the origins and evolution of empathy in the animal kingdom, showing that dolphins are not only intelligent creatures, but also beings capable of compassion.

Fact 63 - Dolphins can change direction quickly

Dolphins are renowned for their exceptional agility in the water, capable of rapid and precise maneuvers. This ability to change direction in an instant is essential to their survival, whether escaping predators, capturing prey or playing among themselves. Their streamlined bodies and powerful musculature enable them to perform these complex movements with remarkable ease.

The flexibility of their spine is a key factor in this agility. Unlike many marine animals, dolphins have a spine that can bend in several directions, facilitating tight, fast turns. This adaptation is particularly useful when hunting fish that move in compact schools, requiring sudden changes of direction so as not to lose sight of their prey.

Their pectoral fins also play a crucial role in their ability to turn quickly. These fins, which act like rudders, enable them to control their trajectory with great precision. By combining subtle movements of their tail and pectoral fins, dolphins can make sharp turns at high speed, an indispensable asset for hunting efficiently or avoiding danger.

Dolphins' smooth, hydrodynamic skin reduces water resistance, facilitating these rapid movements. Micro-ridules on their skin help channel the water around their bodies, enabling them to maintain high speed while retaining exceptional maneuverability. This combination of speed and agility makes dolphins formidable in their aquatic environment.

These skills are not only vital to their survival, but also contribute to their reputation as graceful and impressive creatures. Watching a dolphin change direction with such fluidity is a fascinating sight, bearing witness to millions of years of adaptive evolution.

Fact 64 - Dolphins rub noses to say hello

Dolphins, those social sea creatures, have developed a fascinating way of greeting each other: they rub their noses. This gesture, which resembles a handshake, is regularly observed among these animals. When two dolphins meet, it's not uncommon to see them approach each other and touch the rostrum, their elongated snout, in what appears to be a friendly, respectful gesture.

This nose-rubbing behavior serves to strengthen the social bonds between members of a group. In dolphins, social relationships are essential to survival and individual well-being. By greeting each other in this way, dolphins establish or reaffirm their connection with others, a crucial aspect of their group life. This gesture can be compared to our own greetings, which go beyond the simple exchange of words and can include an affective dimension.

Nose rubbing in dolphins is not simply an act of recognition, but also a means of exchanging information. Thanks to their highly developed sense of touch, these animals can sense subtle variations in each other's skin, which could indicate state of health or mood. What's more, this close interaction enables the dolphins to pick up chemical or electromagnetic signals emitted by their fellow creatures, reinforcing their mutual understanding.

This gesture, while seemingly simple, demonstrates the complexity of social interaction in dolphins. It shows just how nuanced these animals are in their communication, and how refined their social behavior is. By rubbing their noses, dolphins perfectly illustrate the importance of social rituals in maintaining the cohesion of their group.

So this simple nose-rubbing gesture is much more than a simple greeting. It reflects a complex marine society, where every interaction contributes to the harmony and stability of the group. By greeting each other in this way, dolphins remind us that communication goes far beyond words, encompassing a range of subtle and meaningful behaviors.

Fact 65 - Dolphins often share their food

Dolphins are renowned for their complex social behavior, and one of the most fascinating aspects is their tendency to share their food. This behavior, rare among marine animals, demonstrates the altruism that characterizes these cetaceans. It is common to observe a dolphin catching a fish, then voluntarily sharing it with other members of its group, including those not directly related to it.

This sharing is not just an act of generosity; it strengthens the social bonds within the group. By sharing their food, dolphins build and maintain relationships of trust and cooperation, essential for collective survival. This practice is particularly common during periods when food is abundant, enabling dolphins to ensure that all members of their group have access to sufficient resources.

The researchers also found that food sharing in dolphins is not limited to a single individual or group. Dolphins belonging to different groups sometimes share prey, suggesting a degree of inter-group recognition and cooperation. This shows that dolphins are capable of sophisticated social behavior, transcending the usual barriers we might expect to see in the animal kingdom.

Dolphin food sharing can also be seen as a means of educating the youngest members of the group. By sharing their catches with young dolphins, adults teach them not only hunting techniques, but also the importance of solidarity and cooperation. This educational behavior is crucial in transmitting the knowledge and skills needed to survive in a sometimes harsh marine environment.

For dolphins, sharing food is much more than a simple act of kindness. It represents a fundamental pillar of their social structure, a means of strengthening bonds, cooperating for survival and ensuring the transmission of knowledge between generations. This behavior perfectly illustrates the highly social and intelligent nature of dolphins, who continue to fascinate us with their complexity and adaptability.

Fact 66 - Dolphins jump to get rid of parasites

Dolphins are often observed jumping out of the water, a behavior which, although spectacular, has practical reasons. One of the main motivations behind these impressive leaps is parasite control. Indeed, when a dolphin leaps out of the water, the impact with the surface as it falls back creates sufficient force to disorientate or detach parasites clinging to its skin.

This jumping behavior serves as a natural "cleansing" method for these cetaceans. Marine parasites, such as crustaceans or small algae, can attach themselves to the dolphin's skin, causing irritation or even infection. By jumping regularly, dolphins manage to reduce the parasite load that could otherwise affect their health and hydrodynamics.

Jumps are often accompanied by twisting movements in the air, increasing the effectiveness of this method. Fact that the dolphins turn on themselves as they fall maximizes the surface area exposed to the water on impact, improving parasite elimination. These twisting jumps are an example of how dolphins use physical behaviors to maintain their well-being.

Observations show that dolphins perform these jumps not only alone, but also in groups. When hunting or socializing, jumps can serve to strengthen social bonds while fulfilling this cleansing function. This collective behavior ensures that each member of the group remains in good health, a crucial factor for the survival and effectiveness of the group as a unit.

Dolphin leaps, although often perceived as a simple game or a demonstration of joy, actually have a significant functional importance. They demonstrate the ingenuity of these marine animals in using their environment and their physical abilities to maintain good health, while ensuring optimal performance in their natural habitat.

Fact 67 - Dolphins avoid polluted areas

Dolphins, as animals that are extremely sensitive to their environment, instinctively avoid polluted marine areas. Their ability to detect changes in water quality enables them to recognize the dangers associated with these areas, such as the presence of chemicals, plastic waste or other pollutants. This ability to avoid contaminated environments is essential to their survival and well-being.

Dolphins use several of their senses to detect pollution. Their highly sensitive skin can sense chemical changes in the water, while their echolocation enables them to identify areas of low prey density, often a sign of pollution. When they perceive warning signals, they prefer to move to safer areas, where water is cleaner and food resources more abundant.

Studies have shown that dolphin populations living near urban coasts, where pollution is more common, tend to move to less contaminated areas. This proves their ability to recognize environmental threats and adapt their behavior accordingly. However, this avoidance strategy does not always fully protect them, as pollution can spread to wider areas, limiting their options.

In cases where dolphins are forced to remain in polluted areas, due to limited food availability or other factors, they can suffer serious consequences, such as health problems linked to toxin accumulation. Scientists have observed high levels of mercury and other toxic substances in the tissues of dolphins living in contaminated areas, underlining the importance of protecting their natural habitat.

Dolphins' ability to avoid polluted areas demonstrates not only their intelligence, but also their crucial role as indicators of the health of marine ecosystems. Their behavior can serve as an early warning to humans of the dangers of ocean pollution, reminding us of the importance of preserving these habitats for the survival of all marine species.

Fact 68 - Dolphins have hidden vestigial limbs

Although perfectly adapted to life in the water, dolphins bear traces of their evolutionary past. These traces are vestigial limbs, bony structures hidden beneath their skin, which are the remains of ancient hind legs. Although no longer functional, these bones bear witness to the fact that dolphin ancestors once lived on land.

By studying the skeleton of a dolphin, we can observe small bony structures that correspond to what would have been the hind legs of a land mammal. These vestigial bones are a fascinating example of evolution, showing how dolphins, as they transitioned from terrestrial to aquatic life, gradually lost the use of their hind limbs. Yet these bones are still present, hidden beneath the skin, and have not completely disappeared.

Scientists are particularly interested in these remains, as they offer clues to the evolutionary history of cetaceans. Fossils of ancient dolphins and their ancestors show creatures with well-developed hind legs, which gradually shrank over the generations. This evolutionary process enabled dolphins to become the fast, agile swimmers we know today, by exchanging their legs for flippers adapted to life in the water.

Although these vestigial limbs play no role in the swimming or other activities of modern dolphins, their presence is a reminder of the animals' land-based origins. Dolphins, like many other species, carry physical reminders of their long evolutionary history, providing a direct link between their distant past and their current life in the oceans.

Dolphin vestigial limbs are not just a curious biological phenomenon, but living proof of evolution in action. They show how, even after millions of years, traces of the past can persist, hidden beneath the surface, while enabling the species to adapt to the new demands of its environment.

Fact 69 - Dolphins can learn sounds from other species

Dolphins are capable of an astonishing feat: they can not only emit a wide range of sounds, but also learn and imitate the sounds of other species. This ability testifies to their great intelligence and cognitive flexibility. For example, studies have shown that dolphins in captivity, interacting with seals or whales, can reproduce the vocalizations of these animals, a behavior that is not simply instinctive, but a matter of conscious learning.

Dolphins' imitation of the sounds of other species is often linked to complex social interactions. In the wild, a dolphin may learn to imitate the calls of a species with which it regularly interacts, which could be a way of facilitating communication or strengthening social bonds. This behavior is particularly fascinating, as it shows that dolphins have a form of social awareness that enables them to recognize and adopt the behaviors of other species.

Scientists are particularly interested in this ability to imitate, as it may also reveal important aspects of how dolphins perceive and understand their environment. By reproducing the sounds of other animals, dolphins show that they do not simply react instinctively to their sound environment, but are capable of a form of active sound analysis and adaptation.

A concrete example of this phenomenon was observed in dolphins in contact with orcas. The dolphins were able to reproduce the specific sounds of the orcas, a feat all the more impressive given that the vocalizations of the two species differ greatly in frequency and complexity. This demonstrates not only the extent of their vocal abilities, but also their desire or need to communicate with different species.

This phenomenon of vocal learning in dolphins offers a fascinating insight into their social life and intelligence. By showing that they can adapt to other species, these animals reveal a complex and flexible facet of their behavior, which continues to amaze researchers and marine life enthusiasts alike.

Fact 70 - Dolphins prefer shallow waters

Dolphins have a marked preference for shallow waters, where they find not only their food, but also an environment conducive to socialization and raising their young. These areas, often close to the coast, offer them a resource-rich habitat, where ocean currents bring an abundance of fish and small invertebrates, their main diet. This abundance of food is essential for these marine mammals, whose fast metabolism requires frequent meals.

Shallow waters also enable dolphins to move with greater agility and speed. Unlike deep water, where pressures increase and movements can be more limited, coastal areas and estuaries offer them an ideal playground for their famous aquatic acrobatics. These environments also enable them to better exploit their echolocation ability, which works more effectively in these conditions to locate their prey.

Dolphins often choose these waters to raise their young, as they offer natural protection from larger predators such as sharks, which generally prefer deeper areas. The relative safety of these habitats plays a crucial role in the survival of young dolphins, which are particularly vulnerable during the first months of their lives. The social group, or "school", that dolphins form in these areas is also a protective factor, reinforcing collective surveillance against danger.

Another advantage of shallow waters is the complex social interactions that take place. Dolphins form tight-knit groups, where social behaviors such as play, cooperative hunting and even displays of affection are commonplace. These behaviors strengthen bonds within the group and are essential to the social cohesion of the dolphins, who rely on close relationships for their survival.

In short, shallow waters are a strategic choice for dolphins, which find the perfect balance between food, safety and social life. These areas offer them everything they need to thrive, which explains their marked preference for these coastal habitats.

Fact 71 - Male dolphins form coalitions

Male dolphins, particularly certain species such as the bottlenose dolphin (Tursiops truncatus), form coalitions, a rare and fascinating behavior in the animal kingdom. These alliances between males are mainly oriented towards cooperation for reproduction, where several males join forces to court and protect fertile females. These coalitions may include two or three males, but sometimes as many as a dozen, working together in a coordinated fashion.

Forming coalitions enables male dolphins to increase their chances of reproductive success. Indeed, by cooperating, they can better defend a female against other competing males. What's more, this group behavior allows them to take turns in guarding and protecting the female, optimizing the effectiveness of their strategy. This type of cooperation is a remarkable example of the social intelligence of dolphins, where the group's long-term benefits take precedence over immediate individual interests.

These coalitions are not only functional for reproduction, they also play a crucial role in the dolphins' social hierarchy. The males who succeed in establishing and maintaining such alliances are often the ones who dominate the group's social structure. These complex relationships extend over many years, testifying to the memory and ability of dolphins to maintain lasting relationships.

Establishing and maintaining these coalitions involves sophisticated communication between the males. They use a set of vocalizations and specific behaviors to coordinate their actions and maintain harmony within the group. This communication is essential to avoid internal conflicts and ensure effective cooperation.

In short, the coalitions formed by male dolphins are a key aspect of their complex social behavior. These alliances demonstrate not only their intelligence, but also their ability to cooperate to achieve common goals, thereby reinforcing their reproductive success and social standing.

Fact 72 - Dolphins love team games

Dolphins are known for their love of play, and among their favorite activities, team games take pride of place. These intelligent, social animals are not content to play alone, but enjoy organizing collective activities, often involving several individuals. These team games are not only a source of entertainment for dolphins, but also a means of affirming and strengthening bonds within the group.

Among the most common team games observed in dolphins are activities such as ball games, where they use floating objects such as seaweed or fish to throw them at each other. These exchanges often take place with remarkable synchronization, demonstrating their sophisticated coordination and communication skills. These games enable dolphins to develop and maintain the social and physical skills essential to their survival.

Dolphin team games are not only a demonstration of physical and social skills, they also play a crucial role in learning. Young dolphins take part in these activities with adults, learning the social codes of the group, refining their hunting and navigation techniques, and developing the solidarity that characterizes these cetaceans. Play is therefore an integral part of their development, both physically and cognitively.

These playful interactions also reveal the creative side of dolphins. They often invent new ways of playing, transforming everyday activities into complex and fun games. For example, they can create waves to surf together, or play hide-and-seek in coral reefs. This creativity in play is a testament to their intelligence and ability to innovate in their natural environment.

Thus, team play in dolphins is not just a pastime, but an essential activity for their well-being, socialization and learning. These behaviors show just how connected these animals are to each other, always looking for new ways to strengthen their bonds and explore the world around them together.

Fact 73 - Dolphins sometimes cooperate with birds to hunt

As ingenious predators, dolphins have developed a fascinating hunting technique that sometimes involves unexpected collaboration with seabirds. This inter-species cooperation is a striking example of dolphins' ability to adapt and use the resources available in their environment to optimize their chances of hunting success.

When a pod of dolphins locates a school of fish, it's not uncommon to see them working in tandem with birds such as gulls or frigate birds. The dolphins chase the fish towards the water's surface, forming a circle or barrier of bubbles. The trapped fish become an easy target for the birds, who dive in for their share of the feast. Meanwhile, dolphins take advantage of the opportunity to capture panicked fish trying to escape.

This joint hunting strategy enables both species to enjoy a meal without having to expend excessive energy. The birds benefit from the concentration of fish at the surface, while the dolphins reduce the dispersion of the school of fish, thus increasing their catch rate. It's a form of natural collaboration in which each participant benefits from the other's presence.

It's important to note that this cooperation is not systematic, but occurs frequently enough to be recognized as adaptive dolphin behavior. This type of interaction demonstrates not only the intelligence of dolphins, but also their ability to observe and understand the behavior of other species to maximize their own success.

By cooperating with birds to hunt, dolphins once again demonstrate their ingenuity and behavioral flexibility. They not only use their own skills, but are also able to integrate the actions of other animals into their survival strategy, illustrating the complexity of their social behavior and their exceptional intelligence.

Fact 74 - Dolphins move to find food

Dolphins are extremely mobile animals, and their movements are often motivated by the search for food. Their habitat can vary considerably according to the availability of food resources, sometimes leading them to travel long distances to ensure constant access to their preferred prey, such as fish or squid.

These movements are often seasonal. For example, certain groups of coastal dolphins migrate to waters richer in prey during the winter months, when food resources become scarce in their native habitat. This ability to travel long distances demonstrates not only their physical endurance, but also their intelligence in adapting to changing environments.

The search for food drives dolphins to explore different sea areas, from coasts to deeper waters. Their ability to navigate efficiently in diverse marine environments is facilitated by their intelligence and echolocation, a sophisticated system that enables them to detect prey even in murky or dark waters. This adaptability enables them to survive in varied and sometimes difficult conditions.

Dolphins move not only to find food for themselves, but also for their groups, strengthening social bonds within the group. These collective movements are often strategically organized, with dolphins working together to locate and capture prey, enhancing their overall efficiency.

By moving to find food, dolphins once again demonstrate their ability to adapt to their environment and ensure the survival of their group. These movements, which can sometimes cover hundreds of kilometers, are essential to maintaining their food supply and general well-being in dynamic marine ecosystems.

Fact 75 - Dolphins clean themselves with sand

Dolphins are known to use ingenious methods to maintain their hygiene, one of the most surprising being the use of sand to clean themselves. Indeed, these marine animals often rub themselves against the sandy ocean floor, an action that enables them to rid themselves of parasites, dead cells and other impurities present on their skin. This behavior, observed mainly in dolphins living in shallow waters, shows just how ingenious these creatures are.

Sand acts as a kind of natural scrub for dolphins. By rubbing against the sandy bottom, they use the granular texture of the sand to exfoliate their skin. This practice is particularly effective in removing unwanted organisms, such as small crustaceans or algae, which may attach themselves to their bodies. Rubbing against the sand also helps stimulate blood circulation under the skin, which can aid tissue regeneration.

This behavior is often observed during periods of rest or after a hunting session. Dolphins may congregate in areas where the seabed is particularly sandy, and spend several minutes rubbing themselves against the ground, as if in a collective bath. This activity can also strengthen social bonds within the group, as it is often accompanied by play and social interaction.

Using sand to clean themselves once again demonstrates the intelligence and adaptability of dolphins. This behavior is not learned, but appears to be instinctive, which makes it all the more fascinating. By using the resources available in their environment in such a clever way, dolphins show that they are capable of taking care of their physical well-being in a way that is quite unique in the animal kingdom.

Thus, cleaning themselves with sand is not only a matter of hygiene for dolphins, it's also a way for them to keep their skin healthy, remain agile and reinforce interactions within their social group. This habit testifies to their ability to use their environment in innovative ways, proving once again their remarkable intelligence.

Fact 76 - Dolphins synchronize their breath with the waves

Dolphins possess a remarkable ability to synchronize their breathing with the waves, a behavior that testifies to their intelligence and adaptation to the marine environment. When swimming at the water's surface, dolphins instinctively adjust their breathing to the rhythm of the waves, enabling them to optimize each breath and minimize the physical effort required to breathe. This synchronization is particularly noticeable when they move in groups, where each dolphin seems perfectly coordinated with the others.

Synchronizing your breathing with the waves is not only a matter of survival, but also of energy efficiency. By timing their breathing to the crests of the waves, dolphins reduce water resistance and save energy, which is essential for these animals that spend a large part of their lives on the move. This skill is all the more important when traveling long distances or escaping predators.

Young dolphins quickly learn this technique by observing adults. From the very first months of their lives, they imitate the movements of their elders, gradually developing the ability to synchronize their breath with the waves. This skill quickly becomes indispensable for keeping pace with the group, especially when moving fast or in rough waters.

This behavior also highlights the incredible ability of dolphins to understand and interact with their environment in real time. Their ability to synchronize their breath with the waves demonstrates an acute awareness of their own body and position in space, indicative of a complex and developed intelligence.

In short, synchronizing breath with waves is a fascinating example of how dolphins adapt to their environment. This skill testifies to their practical intelligence and ability to maximize energy efficiency in an environment where every detail counts for survival.

Fact 77 - Dolphins love to play hide-and-seek

Dolphins are known for their playfulness, and one of their favorite games is hide-and-seek. This playful behavior, observed both in the wild and in captivity, reveals not only their intelligence, but also their taste for complex social interactions. When playing hide-and-seek, dolphins use their environment, hiding behind rocks, in seaweed, or diving suddenly to escape the sight of their companions.

The game of hide-and-seek in dolphins is not only fun, it also serves to strengthen bonds within the group. By chasing and searching for each other, dolphins improve their coordination and communication. Their high-pitched calls and whistles, used to maintain contact, become essential in this game, enabling them to locate their friends while remaining hidden.

Young dolphins quickly learn the rules of the game by imitating adults. From their very first weeks, they begin to explore potential hiding places and to understand the sound signals emitted by their fellow dolphins. This learning phase is crucial to their development, as it enables them to develop social and cognitive skills that will be essential throughout their lives.

Hide-and-seek also offers dolphins an excellent opportunity to practice their agility and speed. These qualities, vital to their survival, are put to the test in this game, where they have to use speed and cunning to evade their pursuers. This type of exercise is particularly beneficial to their physical development, keeping them fit and having fun at the same time.

In short, dolphin hide-and-seek is much more than just a recreational activity. It's a way for them to strengthen their social skills, hone their communication skills and maintain their physical fitness, while expressing their inquisitive and mischievous nature.

Fact 78 - Dolphins can dive up to 300 meters

Although often seen at the surface, dolphins are also excellent divers, capable of descending to depths of 300 meters. This impressive ability enables them to explore food-rich areas, where they can capture prey that is difficult for other marine animals to access. These deep dives reveal the dolphins' ability to adapt to varied environments, demonstrating their endurance and resilience.

To achieve such dives, dolphins have developed several physiological adaptations. One of the most remarkable is their ability to slow down their heart rate, thus reducing oxygen consumption during prolonged dives. What's more, their bodies are designed to withstand the increased pressure of the deep sea. Their ribcage, for example, is flexible enough to withstand variations in pressure, which is essential to prevent internal injury.

The depth to which a dolphin can dive depends largely on the species and the individual. For example, Risso's dolphins, a particularly robust species, are among those able to dive the deepest. These dives enable them to reach the giant squid, one of their favorite prey, which live at these depths. These hunting behaviors demonstrate the ingenuity of dolphins in their quest for food.

Human divers lucky enough to observe dolphins at these depths testify to the grace with which they move, even in the most hostile environments. They use echolocation to navigate in the near-total darkness of the abyss, an ability that enables them to detect prey and avoid obstacles. This technique, which involves emitting clicks and interpreting echoes, is vital to their survival in these depths.

These dives are not only a demonstration of their adaptability, but also a testament to the incredible diversity of habitats that dolphins can explore. Their ability to dive so deeply is further proof of their intelligence and capacity to adapt to extreme conditions, confirming their place among the most fascinating of marine creatures.

Fact 79 - Dolphins live in waters all over the world

Dolphins, those fascinating marine mammals, populate the world's oceans and seas. Their global distribution reflects their incredible adaptability to different marine environments, whether tropical, temperate or even cold. Dolphins can be seen both near and far offshore, in pelagic zones far from land, demonstrating their ability to thrive in a variety of conditions.

Whether in the Atlantic, Pacific, Indian or Mediterranean Seas, dolphins find their place in a wide variety of marine ecosystems. For example, the bottlenose dolphin, one of the best-known species, is particularly cosmopolitan. It inhabits the temperate waters of the North Atlantic as well as the tropical lagoons of the Caribbean. Other species, such as the Amazonian dolphin, prefer the fresh waters of rivers, showing that some dolphins are not restricted to marine environments.

The different habitats in which dolphins live greatly influence their lifestyle and diet. In cold waters, where food resources may be more dispersed, dolphins have to travel greater distances to feed. Conversely, in tropical regions, where biodiversity is rich, they find prey more easily, enabling them to stay closer to shore. This ability to adapt is essential to their survival in a constantly changing world.

Their presence in so many different regions also demonstrates the importance of dolphins to the health of marine ecosystems. As predators, they play a crucial role in maintaining the balance of fish populations and other marine creatures. Their absence or decline in certain areas could upset this balance, showing just how essential they are to marine biodiversity.

So wherever you are in the world, chances are dolphins aren't far away, swimming beneath the waves and participating in the complex life of the oceans. Their ability to thrive in such diverse environments is one of the many reasons they continue to captivate and inspire humans through the ages.

Fact 80 - Dolphins can use air breaths as weapons

Dolphins are not only intelligent, but also ingenious in the way they interact with their environment. One of their most fascinating techniques is to blow powerful jets of air underwater, a method they use as a weapon to disorient or capture prey. These high-speed blasts of air create bubbles that disrupt the vision and movements of fish, making them easier to capture.

This behavior has been observed in several dolphin species, notably bottlenose dolphins, which hunt in groups and coordinate their attacks to maximize the effectiveness of this technique. By blowing air strategically, they sometimes form a "net" of bubbles around their prey, enclosing them in a restricted space. This strategy enables them to concentrate the fish in a single area, where they can then feed easily.

The use of air breaths as a weapon testifies to the adaptability of dolphins to their environment. These marine mammals have evolved to take advantage of their anatomy and respiratory capacity to influence their environment in unique ways. Unlike other predators that rely on brute force, dolphins use their intelligence and ability to manipulate water to hunt more effectively.

Air bubbles are not only used against prey, but also as a means of defense. Faced with predators like sharks, dolphins can create bubbles to disorientate or ward them off. This defensive behavior once again demonstrates their ability to use unconventional means to protect themselves and their group members.

In short, dolphins' ability to use air breaths as a weapon shows just how ingenious and adaptable they are. Their mastery of this hunting and defense technique testifies to their intelligence and in-depth understanding of the environment in which they evolve.

Fact 81 - Dolphins swim in spirals to hunt

Dolphins, known for their remarkable intelligence, use a variety of hunting strategies, one of the most spectacular of which is the spiral swim. This technique involves swimming in ever-tighter circles around a school of fish. By creating this spiral movement, the dolphins generate a vortex that disorients and compacts the fish in the center of the spiral, making them easier to capture.

This method is particularly effective in deep water, where dolphins can circle their prey at different heights, preventing any escape. In groups, dolphins coordinate to perfect this technique, each playing a precise role to maximize hunting efficiency. This coordination highlights their ability to work as a team and adapt their methods to suit the situation.

One of the fascinating aspects of this technique is the way it relies on echolocation. Dolphins use the sound waves they emit to "see" their surroundings and adjust their position in the spiral. This enables them to track fish movements in real time, adjusting their speed and the size of the circles to keep their prey trapped.

Observations have shown that this spiral hunting technique is transmitted from generation to generation, with young dolphins learning by imitating adults. This transfer of knowledge within groups underlines the importance of social learning in dolphins, a trait also found in other intelligent species such as primates.

In short, spiral swimming for hunting demonstrates once again the complexity of dolphin behavior. This strategy is not only a testament to their intelligence, but also to their ability to collaborate, adapt to their environment and transmit knowledge within their community.

Fact 82 - Dolphins can see in color

Contrary to popular belief, dolphins don't just see in black and white. Their vision is actually more complex, allowing them to perceive certain colors. Although their ability to see colors is not as well-developed as in humans, dolphins have photoreceptors in their eyes that enable them to distinguish certain wavelengths of light, notably in the blue and green spectrum.

Color perception in dolphins is particularly useful in their aquatic environment. Blue and green hues are predominant in oceans and seas, and this visual ability enables them to better spot contrasts and the movements of their prey in the water. For example, a silver fish might be more visible to a dolphin thanks to this color vision, especially in shallow waters where light penetration is greater.

However, dolphins don't perceive all the colors we humans do. They lack certain types of cones in their retinas, which prevents them from seeing colors such as red. This limitation is compensated for by their excellent underwater vision and their ability to use echolocation to detect objects and prey, even in low-light conditions.

Studies have shown that color vision in dolphins also varies according to the species and environments in which they live. For example, dolphins living in rougher waters or at different depths may have developed slightly distinct visual abilities to adapt to their respective habitats.

In short, color vision in dolphins, although limited compared to that of humans, plays a crucial role in their survival. It enables them to better understand and interact with their aquatic environment, demonstrating once again their remarkable adaptation to marine life.

Fact 83 - Dolphins exchange information while swimming

Dolphins are extremely social animals, and their communication is not limited to sounds and whistles. As they swim together, they also exchange important information through their movements and behavior. This subtle form of communication enables them to coordinate their actions, whether hunting, exploring or maintaining group cohesion.

When swimming in groups, dolphins often synchronize their movements, enabling them to transmit information on the direction to take or the presence of prey. For example, a sudden change in speed or direction may signal to other members of the group that a fish has been spotted. This coordination is essential to their survival, especially when hunting fast-moving schools of fish.

Tail movements, sharp turns and even the way they dive or emerge from the water can also be means of communication. These signals are all the more effective when accompanied by characteristic dolphin sounds, such as whistles, clicks or pops. Each member of the group can thus understand what's going on around them, even without direct visual contact with the others.

Researchers have observed that this non-verbal communication is particularly developed in dolphins living in waters where visibility is reduced. In these environments, visual and sound signals complement each other to enable dolphins to stay in contact and avoid danger while optimizing their hunt.

This ability to exchange information while swimming demonstrates the intelligence and social complexity of dolphins. It highlights their remarkable adaptation to group life in an environment where effective communication is often the key to survival.

Fact 84 - Dolphins care for orphaned babies

Dolphins are renowned for their highly developed social behavior, and this includes a particularly touching aspect: their tendency to care for orphaned young within their group. When a juvenile dolphin loses its mother, it is not abandoned to its fate. Other members of the group, often females, take over to ensure that the calf receives the attention and care it needs to survive.

This behavior has been observed on several occasions by researchers. For example, in some dolphin communities, a female may adopt an orphaned calf, feeding and protecting it as if it were her own. This gesture of solidarity is crucial, as the first months of a dolphin's life are crucial to its physical and social development.

The females who care for the orphans often include them in their own daily activities, such as foraging and social play. This enables the young dolphin to learn essential survival skills, while benefiting from the protection of the group. This learning by observation and participation is a key component of the dolphins' social life.

In addition to females, male dolphins can also take part in this collective care, protecting the young orphan from predators or potential dangers. This cooperation within the group demonstrates once again the importance of social bonds among dolphins, where the well-being of each individual is everyone's concern.

This ability to care for orphaned pups reflects not only dolphins' intelligence, but also their profound empathy. They are capable of recognizing the distress of another and reacting in a way that ensures the survival of the group as a whole, thus strengthening the bonds that unite these extraordinary animals.

Fact 85 - Using seagrass to attract females

Male dolphins have developed surprising strategies to attract the attention of females, and one of the most intriguing is the use of sea grass. This behavior has been observed notably in bottlenose dolphins (Tursiops truncatus), where males pick up sprigs of seagrass and proudly display them to seduce a potential mate.

During courtship, these males swim with sea grasses in their mouths or carefully place them on their bodies, creating a sort of natural finery. This behavior is often accompanied by other gestures, such as jumps or graceful movements, which add to the demonstration of their physical abilities and creativity. The use of objects in the context of seduction is quite rare in the animal kingdom, which makes this practice all the more fascinating.

Researchers believe that this behavior may be a way for males to show their resourcefulness and ingenuity, qualities that would be valued by females. Females are more likely to choose a partner who demonstrates such skills, as they indicate an ability to protect and nurture future offspring.

Interactions between males during these demonstrations can also be intense. Some male dolphins compete for the best herbs or use them in the most impressive way possible. This not only reinforces their position in the social hierarchy, but also increases their chances of being chosen by a female.

This behavior shows just how intelligent and adaptive dolphins are, able to use their environment in innovative ways to achieve their goals. The use of seagrass to seduce females is a perfect example of the complexity of social interactions in dolphins and their ability to use objects as tools in their daily lives.

Fact 86 - Dolphins are expert navigators

Dolphins are renowned for their incredible ability to navigate the ocean, a skill that places them among the best navigators in the animal kingdom. Thanks to their natural sonar, known as echolocation, they can detect and analyze sounds bouncing off underwater objects, enabling them to navigate with unrivalled precision, even in the murkiest or darkest waters.

This ability is essential to their survival, enabling them to avoid obstacles, locate schools of fish or find their way back on long migratory journeys. Dolphins can travel hundreds of kilometers in a precise direction, demonstrating an astonishing mastery of their marine environment. This ability to navigate with such finesse is all the more impressive when one considers the vast expanses of water in which they evolve.

Studies have shown that dolphins also use ocean currents, the Earth's magnetic fields, and even underwater geographical landmarks to navigate. For example, some dolphins follow reef lines or underwater mountain ranges to reach their preferred hunting or breeding grounds. This sophisticated understanding of their environment demonstrates not only their intelligence, but also their ability to fully exploit the resources of their habitat.

Their ability to navigate is not only vital to their own survival, but also to their role in the marine ecosystem. As predators, they regulate fish populations and maintain the ecological balance. By moving so efficiently, they can exploit different hunting grounds while avoiding more dangerous predators such as sharks.

Ultimately, dolphins illustrate how nature can equip its creatures with impressive tools to navigate and survive in complex environments. Their navigational skills are a testament to their evolutionary adaptation and unique place in the marine world.

Fact 87 - Dolphins can recognize human faces

Dolphins are renowned for their exceptional intelligence, and among their many skills, their ability to recognize human faces stands out in particular. Thanks to their visual memory and keen sense of observation, dolphins can not only identify different individuals, but also remember them over long periods of time. This ability is often observed in interactions between captive dolphins and their caregivers.

Studies have shown that dolphins use a combination of their eyesight, which is particularly good underwater, and their sonar to identify specific facial features. Contrary to what one might think, this recognition is not limited to shapes or silhouettes; dolphins appear to be able to distinguish the complex details of human faces, suggesting a form of recognition similar to that of primates.

The researchers also observed that dolphins show preferences for certain human faces, reacting more enthusiastically when they see people they know well. These reactions include jumping, whistling, or friendly approaches, underlining the importance of social bonds for these animals. This face recognition could play an important role in the formation of lasting relationships with humans, strengthening cooperation between dolphins and their caretakers.

This fascinating ability testifies to the extraordinary intelligence of dolphins and their ability to adapt to complex environments, including those shared with humans. Their ability to remember and distinguish between human faces shows that, although they are marine creatures, dolphins share certain advanced cognitive abilities also found in land mammals.

In short, dolphins' recognition of human faces is further evidence of their cognitive complexity and ability to interact in sophisticated ways with their environment and with humans. This reinforces the idea that dolphins are not only intelligent animals, but also social beings capable of developing meaningful bonds beyond their own species.

Fact 88 - Dolphins like to play with fish

Dolphins are known for their inquisitive and playful nature, and one of the most fascinating aspects of their behavior is their habit of playing with fish. Contrary to what you might think, these interactions are not always related to hunting or feeding. Often, dolphins capture a fish not to eat it immediately, but to engage in a kind of game where they release it and catch it again and again.

This behavior has been observed in various dolphin populations around the world. In tropical waters, for example, dolphins have been seen throwing fish in the air or chasing them in tight circles. These games appear to be a form of entertainment, but they can also help dolphins perfect their hunting techniques and strengthen social bonds within their group.

Young dolphins, in particular, are often the most playful and use these interactions with fish to develop their skills. They learn to coordinate their movements, anticipate the reactions of their prey, and work as a team. These games are essential for their development and adaptation to the marine environment.

However, this playful side of dolphins is not limited to youngsters. Adults also take part in these games, and it's common to see several dolphins playing together with a single fish. This type of interaction demonstrates just how social and intelligent dolphins are, capable of turning a simple hunting opportunity into a fun, collective activity.

Dolphins' love of playing with fish is a testament to their behavioral complexity. These games are not only a pastime, but also a demonstration of their intelligence, their curiosity, and their need for mental and social stimulation in an environment where survival demands sharpened skills.

Fact 89 - Dolphins use echolocation to avoid predators

Dolphins possess a keen sense of echolocation, a vital tool not only for hunting, but also for detecting and avoiding predators. This ability enables them to emit sounds that travel underwater, bounce off objects or creatures around them, then return as echoes. By interpreting these echoes, dolphins can determine the size, shape, distance and even speed of movement of elements in their environment.

When dolphins perceive a potential predator, such as a shark, echolocation gives them a detailed picture of the threat. This hyper-developed sense enables them to detect the presence of predators long before they are visible to the naked eye. Depending on this information, the dolphins may then decide to flee, regroup to defend themselves, or seek shelter in areas less accessible to predators.

Echolocation is so precise that dolphins can even tell the difference between a shark and other less dangerous fish, based on the predator's body shape and density. This ability is particularly crucial in waters with reduced visibility, such as deep or murky waters, where relying on sight alone would be insufficient to ensure their safety.

Dolphins not only detect predators, they also use echolocation to coordinate their movements as a group. By emitting clicks and receiving responses from other members of the group, they can quickly organize themselves to react to a threat. This sophisticated communication allows them to protect the most vulnerable individuals, such as young dolphins, by placing them at the center of the group.

Echolocation is much more than a simple navigation or hunting tool for dolphins. It's a sophisticated defense mechanism that gives them a crucial advantage in the ocean, where predators can appear at any moment. Thanks to this ability, dolphins manage to survive and thrive in often hostile marine environments.

Fact 90 - Dolphins can detect heartbeats

Dolphins have an exceptional ability to detect the heartbeats of other animals, including humans. This amazing skill is due to their use of echolocation, a complex mechanism that enables them to "see" with sound. By emitting ultrasonic clicks and interpreting the returning echoes, dolphins can perceive not only the external structure of a body, but also internal details such as heart rate.

This phenomenon has been observed in situations where dolphins interact with humans or other marine animals. For example, during interaction sessions in dolphinariums, some dolphins have been seen to approach the thorax of humans in a very targeted manner, as if they were "listening" to their heartbeat. This ability gives them a special sensitivity that goes beyond simple communication or identification of objects in their environment.

The detection of heartbeats is made possible by the finesse of their echolocation. The ultrasonic sounds they emit penetrate body tissues and are able to bounce off moving surfaces, such as heart valves or blood flow. This enables them to pick up subtle variations in heart rate, which could be a tool for assessing the state of stress or health of another living being.

In their natural environment, this skill could have a social or survival function, enabling them to judge the state of their fellow fish or other marine creatures. For example, they could detect whether a fish is weakened or ill by sensing anomalies in its heartbeat, helping them to select their prey more effectively.

Dolphins' ability to detect heartbeats illustrates once again the incredible sophistication of their echolocation system. This unique ability gives them an extra sense of interaction with their environment and the other creatures that populate it, giving them a fine, detailed awareness of their surroundings.

Fact 91 - Dolphins sing to calm their young

Dolphins are known for their wide repertoire of sounds, but one of the most fascinating aspects of their communication is their ability to "sing" to calm their young. These songs, or specific vocalizations, are used by dolphin mothers to soothe their offspring when they are agitated or frightened. These soft, rhythmic sounds, often described as melodious whistles, have a soothing effect on young dolphins, similar to human lullabies.

This behavior has been observed in various situations where young dolphins show signs of distress. For example, after a stressful event such as an encounter with a predator or temporary separation from the group, mothers emit these soothing songs. Scientists believe that these sounds are not only comforting, but also serve to strengthen the bond between mother and calf, fostering a sense of security and protection.

The ability of dolphins to modulate their sounds according to the emotional needs of their young bears witness to their great social sensitivity. This vocal communication is an essential tool for maintaining cohesion and harmony within the group, particularly in the early stages of a dolphin's life. The sounds emitted are specific to each mother and can even be recognized by other dolphins in the group, underlining the importance of vocal recognition in their society.

It is also interesting to note that this behavior is not limited to mothers and offspring. Members of the same group can use similar vocalizations to calm or reassure a fellow member in a stressful situation. This demonstrates the empathy and social intelligence of dolphins, capable of perceiving the emotions of their peers and responding appropriately.

Ultimately, these soothing songs are further evidence of the complexity of social interactions in dolphins. They show how these animals use their vocal abilities not only to communicate practical information, but also to maintain deep emotional relationships with members of their group.

Fact 92 - Dolphins use stones to scratch themselves

Dolphins never cease to amaze with their ingenuity and ability to use objects in their environment to meet their needs. One of the most fascinating behaviors observed in these cetaceans is the use of stones to scratch themselves. This behavior once again demonstrates their intelligence and ability to find practical solutions to everyday problems, such as the need to relieve itching or eliminate parasites.

Dolphins are often seen rubbing against rocks or stones at the bottom of the water. This behavior seems to be an effective way for them to get rid of irritants on their skin, such as algae or parasites. By using rough surfaces, they manage to scrape hard-to-reach areas, providing immediate relief. This kind of activity underlines not only their ingenuity, but also their understanding of how to use natural tools.

This behavior has been documented by researchers, who have observed groups of dolphins deliberately choosing rocky areas to scratch themselves. Dolphins seem to have a preference for certain stones or rocks, which they regularly use for this task. This is further evidence of their ability to learn and memorize specific places in their environment where they can find what they need.

This scratching is not limited to individual needs. Dolphins are social animals, and it's not uncommon to see several individuals scratching simultaneously on the same stone or in the same area. This can even become a social moment, when dolphins come together to scratch and strengthen their social bonds at the same time. This aspect of their lives shows how every action in the world of dolphins can have several levels of significance, ranging from a simple physical need to a more complex social interaction.

In conclusion, dolphins' use of stones for scratching is another fascinating example of their intelligence and adaptability. It shows not only their ability to solve practical problems, but also to integrate these solutions into their social lives, making every interaction an opportunity to enrich their relationships within the group.

Fact 93 - Dolphins modulate their breathing according to depth

Dolphins, masters of the oceans, possess an astonishing ability to modulate their breathing according to the depth at which they dive. This adaptation is essential to their survival and enables them to explore the different layers of the ocean efficiently. Their respiratory system is incredibly flexible, automatically adjusting to optimize oxygen use according to the specific needs of each dive.

When a dolphin dives to greater depths, it considerably reduces its breathing rate. This modulation is crucial, as it conserves the oxygen stored in the lungs while minimizing energy consumption. This precise breath control also avoids pressure-related risks, such as gas embolisms, which can be fatal at great depths.

Scientists have observed that dolphins are able to remain apneic for long periods, in part by modulating the volume of air inhaled before the dive. They adjust the amount of air according to the duration and depth of the planned dive. For example, for a short, shallow dive, they'll take a normal inhalation, but for a deep dive, they'll fill their lungs to the maximum.

This ability to modulate breath is not limited to oxygen management. It also plays a crucial role in echolocation, a tool dolphins use to navigate and hunt underwater. By controlling their breath, dolphins can emit sounds at optimal frequencies to detect objects or prey at different depths, ensuring effective communication and hunting.

In short, depth-dependent breath modulation is a testament to dolphins' ingenuity and adaptation to the challenges of marine life. This ability enables them not only to survive, but also to thrive in a variety of marine environments, from shallow waters to mysterious abysses.

Fact 94 - Dolphins communicate with snapping sounds

Dolphins, social animals par excellence, use a wide range of sounds to communicate with each other. Among these sounds, snapping occupies a special place. These dry noises, produced by snapping their jaws, are an essential tool in their complex language, enabling them to convey crucial information in their daily lives. Clacking sounds are produced at a variety of frequencies, making this communication adaptable to different situations.

These clicks are used not only to transmit messages, but also to find their way around their environment thanks to echolocation. By emitting these sounds and listening to the returning echoes, dolphins can detect objects, prey or even obstacles several meters away. This process is remarkably accurate, comparable to natural sonar, and enables them to navigate with ease even in murky or dark waters.

Dolphins modulate these clicks according to the context. For example, they may intensify the frequency and speed of their snapping sounds when hunting, to better locate their prey. On the other hand, during social interactions, these sounds become more spaced out and melodious, facilitating communication with other members of the group. Each dolphin has a unique sound signature, rather like a human voice, which enables them to recognize each other.

These clicking sounds also play an important role in the social hierarchy of dolphins. When interacting, arguing or playing, these sounds can be used to signal intent, assert status or strengthen bonds between individuals. Dolphins also use these sounds to alert other dolphins to danger, demonstrating their ability to work as a team to ensure the group's survival.

In short, snapping is not just a noise for dolphins, but a sophisticated means of communication, capable of conveying a variety of messages adapted to each situation. These sounds, emitted with precision and intention, testify to the remarkable intelligence of these marine mammals and their ability to live together in a harmonious, organized society.

Fact 95 - Dolphins can live in icy waters

Contrary to the idea that dolphins only prefer warm waters, some dolphin species are perfectly adapted to living in icy waters. These dolphins, like those found in subarctic regions, have specific adaptations that enable them to survive in extreme conditions. Their thick layer of blubber is one of these key adaptations. It insulates them from the cold, maintaining a stable body temperature despite the surrounding icy waters.

Dolphins living in these cold regions have also developed a unique behavior to prevent ice from forming on their skin. They often swim close to the surface and make constant movements to prevent ice from attaching to their bodies. This behavior enables them to stay mobile and avoid becoming trapped under the ice, where access to air would be limited.

In addition to their physical adaptations, these dolphins modify their diet according to the seasons and the availability of prey. In winter, when the waters are ice-covered, they may feed on fish living under the ice or near cracks where the water remains open. Their ability to hunt in these difficult conditions demonstrates their incredible resilience and intelligence.

Cold-water dolphins have also learned to use icy conditions to their advantage. For example, they can use the ice as shelter from predators, such as orcas, which are less agile in ice-covered waters. This ingenious use of their environment shows just how well adapted these dolphins are to their icy habitat.

Finally, despite the challenges posed by icy waters, these dolphins continue to form strong, close-knit social groups, collaborating to hunt and protect one another. Their ability to survive and thrive in such harsh environments is a testament to their formidable adaptability and intelligence, making them every bit as fascinating as their tropical counterparts.

Fact 96 - Dolphins love to race each other

Dolphins are particularly playful animals, and one of their favorite activities is racing each other. These friendly competitions not only strengthen bonds within the group, but also demonstrate the agility and speed of these marine mammals. Races generally take place on the surface of the water, where the dolphins launch themselves at full speed, making spectacular leaps and splashes.

These races are not just a means of entertainment. They also allow the dolphins to train their fast swimming skills, essential for escaping predators or capturing prey. During these competitions, dolphins can reach impressive speeds of up to 40 km/h, using the full power of their tails to propel themselves.

The social nature of dolphins is reflected in the way they participate in these races. They like to gather in teams or pairs, and it's not uncommon to see several dolphins synchronizing their movements to swim together. This sense of togetherness shows just how important social relationships are to them, even in playful activities.

These racing games are also an opportunity for young dolphins to learn from adults. By observing the more experienced, the youngsters perfect their swimming technique and develop their reflexes. As for the adults, they seem to appreciate the enthusiasm of the youngsters and encourage them by accompanying them in their sprints.

Dolphin races are not only a demonstration of strength and speed, they also strengthen the social bonds within the group, while allowing the youngest to develop in a playful and stimulating environment. These playful moments illustrate the dolphins' joie de vivre and incredible community spirit.

Fact 97 - Dolphins can modulate their whistles

Dolphins have an incredible ability to modulate their whistles, enabling them to communicate in sophisticated and precise ways. These whistles are not simply uniform sounds, but can vary in frequency, duration and intensity, offering a wide range of sonic nuances. Each dolphin is capable of producing a unique whistle, often called a "signature whistle", which functions like a proper name, facilitating identification between group members.

The modulation of whistles enables dolphins to transmit complex information. For example, they can signal their position, express an emotion, or alert the group to the presence of danger. These subtle variations in whistling show just how advanced communication between dolphins is, almost comparable to a language. The researchers discovered that dolphins can even imitate the whistles of other individuals, demonstrating a vocal learning capacity similar to that observed in humans.

This ability to modulate whistles is not only useful for social interaction, but also plays a crucial role when hunting. Dolphins use their modulated whistles to coordinate group movements, ensuring that everyone plays their part when circling prey. The nuances of the whistles help to maintain synchronization and adjust strategy in real time, which is essential for a successful hunt.

Dolphins also adapt their whistling to the acoustic environment. For example, in noisy waters, they tend to increase the frequency of their whistles to make themselves heard above the ambient noise. This flexibility once again demonstrates the intelligence and adaptability of these marine animals. They can even use these modulations to soothe members of their group, thus strengthening social bonds.

Dolphins never cease to amaze with their ability to modulate their whistles, making their communication not only rich and diverse, but also incredibly effective. This unique talent further reinforces the idea that dolphins are exceptionally intelligent creatures, capable of adapting to a wide range of situations thanks to their vocal skills.

Fact 98 - Dolphins prefer clear water for hunting

As seasoned hunters, dolphins show a marked preference for clear waters when they go in search of food. This preference is explained by the better visibility offered by these environments, making it easier for them to spot their prey, whether fish or squid. In these clear waters, dolphins can use their sight to complement their echolocation, giving them a considerable advantage when hunting.

Clear waters, typical of shallow coastal areas or coral reefs, also enable dolphins to coordinate their hunting efforts with greater precision. They can see the movements of other dolphins and adjust their own actions accordingly. For example, during a group hunt, one dolphin may block the escape of a school of fish while the others surround them, forming a sort of living net.

This preference for clear water is particularly evident in certain species of dolphin, such as the bottlenose dolphin, often observed near shores with crystal-clear water. Here, dolphins can exploit ideal conditions to practice sophisticated hunting techniques, such as forming mud rings or bubbles to encircle their prey. These ingenious methods are most effective when visibility is excellent, underlining the importance of clear waters for these animals.

In addition to facilitating hunting, clear waters also enable dolphins to better monitor their surroundings for potential dangers, such as sharks. This dual function of safety and feeding efficiency explains why dolphins prefer these habitats. Turbid waters, on the other hand, can reduce their field of vision and expose them more to predators, while making it more difficult to locate their food.

Dolphins' preference for clear water when hunting is a striking example of their ability to optimize their environment to maximize their chances of survival. This strategy reveals not only their intelligence, but also their incredible adaptability to different marine habitats.

Fact 99 - Dolphins exchange information about predators

Dolphins have a remarkable ability to communicate vital information with each other, particularly concerning the presence of predators in their environment. This ability is crucial to their survival, especially in waters where sharks, their main predators, frequently prowl. Dolphins use a combination of whistles, clicks and gestures to signal the presence of a threat to their fellow dolphins, enabling a rapid collective response.

When a dolphin detects a shark, it may emit a distinctive sound signal that immediately alerts the rest of the group. This signal, often accompanied by behavioral changes such as fleeing or defensive regrouping, enables the other members to become aware of the danger and adopt protective measures. This rapid and effective communication is an example of how dolphins use their intelligence to maximize their chances of survival.

What's more, dolphins don't just warn those around them. They are also capable of memorizing information about predators, such as their hunting habits or the areas where they are most often observed. This knowledge is then shared within the group, contributing to a collective defense strategy. For example, a group of dolphins may avoid a certain area where a shark has been spotted frequently, thus reducing the risk of attack.

The exchange of information on predators is particularly developed in dolphins living in areas where sharks are abundant. These dolphins develop sophisticated methods not only to detect predators, but also to monitor and avoid them. This ability to exchange complex information shows just how socially and cognitively advanced dolphins are.

Ultimately, communication between dolphins regarding predators is an essential aspect of their group life. It strengthens their social cohesion while increasing their resilience in the face of danger, demonstrating once again the complexity and ingenuity of these fascinating marine creatures.

Fact 100 - Adjust your behavior to your environment

Dolphins are particularly adaptable animals, able to modify their behavior according to environmental conditions. This ability to adapt is crucial to their survival, enabling them to thrive in habitats as diverse as shallow coastal waters, rivers and vast oceans. Their intelligence and powers of observation play a central role in these adjustments, which range from foraging to predator avoidance.

For example, in shallow waters where food resources may be limited, dolphins adjust their hunting strategy. They may use specific techniques, such as hunting in groups to surround fish and maximize their chances of capture. On the other hand, in deeper waters where prey is more dispersed, they prefer to hunt individually or in small groups, adjusting their approach to suit local conditions.

Dolphins' social behavior also varies according to their environment. In areas where predators, such as sharks, are abundant, dolphins tend to form larger groups for mutual protection. These groups, called shoals, can be very fluid, with dolphins joining or leaving the group according to perceived danger. In safer environments, on the other hand, dolphins may form smaller groups or even spend time alone.

Dolphins' interactions with humans are also influenced by their environment. In areas where they are regularly in contact with fishermen or tourists, dolphins can become more curious and interactive. They adapt their behavior to take advantage of the opportunities offered by these interactions, for example by following fishing boats to retrieve discarded fish. On the other hand, in less-frequented areas, they tend to be more wary and keep their distance.

Finally, dolphins show great flexibility in their communication depending on the environment. They modulate their vocalizations according to acoustic conditions, such as water depth or the presence of ambient noise, to ensure that their signals are well received by other members of the group.

Conclusion

You've just read 100 amazing facts about dolphins, the creatures that have inhabited our oceans and fascinated mankind for centuries. These intelligent, sociable animals may have surprised you with their complexity and ingenuity. Beyond their playful image, dolphins reveal a world rich in emotions, strategies and unique behaviors that make them much more than mere marine mammals.

Through these Facts, you've been able to explore the many facets of dolphin life: their ability to communicate, cooperate, and even bond with other species, including humans. Their adaptability and intelligence are traits that set them apart in the animal kingdom, and you now have a better understanding of what makes these creatures so special.

But this book is also a reminder of the importance of preserving their natural habitat. Dolphins, like so many other marine species, face many challenges, including pollution, overfishing and climate change. As you get to know them better, you'll realize the need to protect these animals and the oceans they inhabit.

Every Fact you discover brings you a little closer to the fascinating and sometimes fragile reality of dolphins. They're not just animals to be admired from afar; they're living beings with whom we share the planet, and they deserve our respect and attention. By protecting them, we also protect the delicate balance of marine ecosystems.

As you finish this book, I hope you'll remember the lessons you've learned and continue to marvel at the beauty and complexity of the marine world. Dolphins are true ambassadors of the oceans, and it's our duty to ensure that they continue to thrive in a world that still offers them the freedom and safety they need.

Quiz

1) How many human commands can a trained dolphin understand?

    a)   20 orders
    b)   40 orders
    c)   60 orders
    d)   80 orders

2) With which other marine species are dolphins known to have friendly relations?

    a)   Sharks
    b)   Jellyfish
    c)   Humpback whales
    d)   Octopuses

3) In the social structure of dolphins, who plays a central role in group organization?

    a)   The strongest males
    b)   The females
    c)   Young dolphins
    d)   The solitary dolphins

4) What technique do dolphins use to chase fish by disorienting them?

    a)   They encircle them with seaweed
    b)   They use rocks to trap them.
    c)   They create a net of bubbles
    d)   They attract them with high-pitched sounds

5) Why do dolphins jump out of the water according to the Fact?

    a)   To show their agility
    b)   To catch insects
    c)   To observe their environment
    d)   To play with the waves

6) What technique do dolphins use to hunt in low-visibility environments?

    a)   Night vision
    b)   Camouflage
    c)   Echolocation
    d)   Telepathic communication

7) What makes dolphin skin particularly sensitive?

    a)   The presence of oily glands
    b)   A thick layer of grease
    c)   A thin layer of epidermis with numerous nerve endings

d) The rough texture of their skin

8) How much fish can a dolphin eat per day to maintain its energy and agility?

a) 5 kg
b) 10 kg
c) 15 kg
d) 20 kg

9) What special sound do dolphins make when they play together?

a) A high-pitched whistle
b) A roar
c) A special laugh
d) A piercing scream

10) How have dolphins repeatedly saved humans from drowning?

a) Shouting to alert rescue workers
b) Pushing them towards the surface or the shore
c) Pulling them by the hair
d) By drawing them to the bottom of the water

11) How do dolphins demonstrate their sense of humor?

a) Keeping quiet when they're having fun
b) Avoid playing with objects
c) Deliberately splashing swimmers to provoke amused reactions
d) Completely ignoring the other dolphins as they play

12) How do dolphins use their coded sounds to communicate?

a) By emitting random, meaningless sounds
b) Using whistles and clicks to form specific "words" or "phrases"
c) By imitating the sounds of other marine animals
d) By communicating solely through gestures without using sounds

13) What social behavior do dolphins display when they share their food?

a) They show their dominance over other group members
b) They strengthen social ties and cooperation within the group
c) They establish individual territories by sharing their food.
d) They train their youngsters to become independent

14) Why do dolphins prefer shallow water?

a) Because they find a greater variety of rare prey there
b) Because these zones are richer in oxygen
c) Because these waters offer protection from predators and an abundance of food

d) Because shallow waters are warmer all year round

15) Why do dolphins rub against the sandy ocean floor?

a) To protect yourself from the cold
b) To sharpen their teeth
c) For cleansing and eliminating parasites
d) To camouflage their scent from predators

16) How do dolphins use the air they breathe underwater?

a) To signal to other dolphins
b) To cool their bodies
c) To disorient or capture prey
d) To purify the water around them

17) How do male dolphins use seagrass during courtship?

a) To build nests
b) For camouflage from predators
c) To attract the attention of females
d) To mark their territory

18) How can dolphins detect the heartbeats of other animals, including humans?

a) Feeling the vibrations in the water
b) Using their exceptional vision
c) By listening to the sounds emitted by the heart
d) Using echolocation to perceive internal movements

19) What adaptation enables dolphins to survive in icy waters?

a) Thick, cold-resistant skin
b) A diet based exclusively on cold-water fish
c) A thick layer of fat called blubber that insulates them from the cold
d) Breathing that filters icy air

20) How do dolphins adjust their behavior in waters where prey is more dispersed?

a) They hunt in larger groups
b) They move into shallow water
c) They hunt individually or in small groups
d) They increase their swimming speed

Answers

1) How many human commands can a trained dolphin understand?

Correct answer: c) 60 orders

2) With which other marine species are dolphins known to have friendly relations?

Correct answer: c) Humpback whales

3) In the social structure of dolphins, who plays a central role in group organization?

Correct answer: b) Females

4) What technique do dolphins use to chase fish by disorienting them?

Correct answer: c) They create a net of bubbles

5) Why do dolphins jump out of the water according to the Fact?

Correct answer: c) To observe their environment

6) What technique do dolphins use to hunt in low-visibility environments?

Correct answer: c) Echolocation

7) What makes dolphin skin particularly sensitive?

Correct answer: c) A thin layer of epidermis with numerous nerve endings

8) How much fish can a dolphin eat per day to maintain its energy and agility?

Correct answer: c) 15 kg

9) What special sound do dolphins make when they play together?

Correct answer: c) A special laugh

10) How have dolphins repeatedly saved humans from drowning?

Correct answer: b) By pushing them towards the surface or the shore.

11) How do dolphins demonstrate their sense of humor?

Correct answer: c) By deliberately splashing the swimmers to provoke amused reactions.

12) How do dolphins use their coded sounds to communicate?

Correct answer: b) By using whistles and clicks to form specific "words" or "phrases".

13) What social behavior do dolphins display when they share their food?

Correct answer: b) They strengthen social ties and cooperation within the group.

14) Why do dolphins prefer shallow water?

Correct answer: c) Because these waters offer protection from predators and an abundance of food.

15) Why do dolphins rub against the sandy ocean floor?

Correct answer: c) To clean and eliminate parasites

16) How do dolphins use the air they breathe underwater?

Correct answer: c) To disorient or capture prey

17) How do male dolphins use seagrass during courtship?

Correct answer: c) To attract the attention of females

18) How can dolphins detect the heartbeats of other animals, including humans?

Correct answer: d) Using echolocation to perceive internal movements

19) What adaptation enables dolphins to survive in icy waters?

Correct answer: c) A thick layer of fat called blubber insulates them from the cold.

20) How do dolphins adjust their behavior in waters where prey is more dispersed?

Correct answer: c) They hunt individually or in small groups.